# About this Learning Guide

## Shmoop Will Make You a Better Lover*
*of Literature, History, Poetry, Life...

Our lively learning guides are written by experts and educators who want to show your brain a good time. Shmoop writers come primarily from Ph.D. programs at top universities, including Stanford, Harvard, and UC Berkeley.

Want more Shmoop? We cover literature, poetry, bestsellers, music, US history, civics, biographies (and the list keeps growing). Drop by our website to see the latest.

## www.shmoop.com

# Table of Contents

# Introduction

## In a Nutshell

Zombies! Black magic! Riots! Rum-soaked Caribbean honeymoon! Squishy bugs! Monkeys!

OK, so we were kidding about the monkeys, but all that other stuff? It's all in Jean Rhys's *Wide Sargasso Sea*, and it's widely considered a *literary classic*. How could this be, you ask?

Jean Rhys first read Charlotte Brontë's *Jane Eyre* in 1907, when she arrived in England as a teenager. As a native of the Caribbean herself, she was "shocked" by Brontë's portrayal of Bertha Mason, Rochester's Creole wife who was locked up in the attic ( Rhys 1999: 144). Nearly fifty years later, Rhys turned the story of Brontë's "madwoman in the attic" into a full-length novel, *Wide Sargasso Sea*, which pretty much established Rhys as one of the greatest novelists in the twentieth century.

*Wide Sargasso Sea* isn't just a prequel, but a significant re-writing of one of the classics of Victorian fiction. Instead of a shrieking specter, we get a psychologically nuanced portrayal of Antoinette (Bertha) Mason, a young white Creole girl coming of age in Jamaica while it was still a British colony. The Caribbean is no longer an exotic afterthought, but a vibrant locale described with an eye trained on its dense social, cultural, and historical landscape. The marriage of Antoinette and Rochester is no longer just a painful back-story, but a stage on which the sexes battle it out for emotional and economic control.

*Wide Sargasso Sea* also alters the historical setting of *Jane Eyre* by pushing the chronology up almost thirty years later in order to take advantage of another foundational moment in Jamaican history, the abolition of slavery in 1834. Setting the novel during this tumultuous period enables Rhys to situate the figure of the white Creole woman in the complex of shifting race relations under British colonial rule.

No wonder, then, that *Wide Sargasso Sea* isn't just a fascinating and entertaining story, but a work that has profoundly impacted the way that readers approach the "great books" of Western literature. The novel challenges us to read these texts critically for the untold stories of characters who are marginalized because they don't fit into the dominant paradigm of what a hero or heroine ought to be.

(Oh, and can you "get" *Wide Sargasso Sea* without having any idea what *Jane Eyre* is about? Absolutely. Can you love *Jane Eyre* and be seduced by *Wide Sargasso Sea* at the same time? Of course – many people do. The beauty of *Wide Sargasso Sea* is that it lets you have it both ways.)

## Why Should I Care?

What do you get when *Lost* meets *Mean Girls*, sprinkled with a little *Night of the Living Dead*, *Pirates of the Caribbean*, and the three *Star Wars* prequels? Welcome to the world of *Wide*

*Sargasso Sea*, with its blend of twisted romance and island mystery, occult magic and literary self-reference.

Let's start with *Lost*. An island where unexplained things happen, where conventional notions of space and time are turned inside out, where you're constantly threatened by "Others" whose intentions remain obscure, where there are constant allusions to literature and philosophy – sounds a lot like Rhys's Caribbean, doesn't it? It might be tough to see balding John Locke stirring up an obeah (or voodoo) potion *à la* Christophine, but both are charismatic characters whose influence comes largely from their claim to know more about how the island operates than everyone else.

Judging by all the prequels out there, you could say that the pre-history of a story can be just as compelling as the story itself. Be it Hannibal Lecter or Indiana Jones, Wolverine, or Yoda, prequels offer the tempting possibility of understanding how a fascinating character works. When they really deliver, like *Wide Sargasso Sea*, they offer another way of enjoying your favorite tale.

But the novel doesn't just tap into some tried-and-true cultural motifs – it relates to some important contemporary social questions as well. Antoinette's struggles with her self-image and her sexuality speak to issues of body image, self-esteem, and even relationship violence that many people face at some point in their lives. And if you've ever been the victim of gossip, you know that even after the gossiper has apologized profusely and attempted to clear the air, the gossip is *out there*, part of the way the world looks at you whether you like it or not. The novel gets at the uncomfortable truth that words can hurt just as much as sticks and stones.

## Book Summary

As Part I opens, Antoinette Cosway is a young girl living with her mother and brother at Coulibri, her family's estate near Spanish Town, Jamaica. With the passage of the Emancipation Act and the death of her father, the family is financially ruined. Moreover, they are ostracized by both the black and white communities on the island. The black community despises them for being former slaveholders, and the white community looks down on them because they are poor, Creole, and, in her mother's case, French. Among the only servants who remain is Christophine, a Martinique woman who is rumored to practice obeah.

Motivated in part by her family's desperate situation, Annette, Antoinette's mother, marries Mr. Mason, a wealthy planter. This marriage, however, only seems to aggravate racial tensions in their neighborhood. One night, rioters burn the house down. The entire family narrowly escapes, all except Antoinette's brother Pierre, who, due to his exposure to the smoke, either dies very soon after. Pierre's death devastates Annette, who goes mad with grief. Mr. Mason sends Annette off to an isolated house to be cared for by a colored couple. Antoinette is sent to live with her aunt Cora in Spanish Town. For a year and a half, Antoinette attends a convent school there. Part I ends with Mr. Mason back in Antoinette's life, insinuating that plans for arranging

her marriage are already under way.

Part II opens with a newly wedded Antoinette and Rochester on their honeymoon in Granbois, the Cosway estate outside Massacre, Dominica. Through a series of flashbacks, we learn that their marriage was arranged by Rochester's father, Mr. Mason, and Richard Mason, Antoinette's stepbrother. After only a month of courtship, Rochester married Antoinette. While at first wary of each other, Antoinette and Rochester grow to trust each other and consummate their marriage.

But the honeymoon is short-lived, as Rochester receives a malicious letter from a man who claims to be Daniel Cosway, Antoinette's stepbrother. The letter alleges that there is a history of sexual degeneracy and mental illness in Antoinette's family, and it also alleges that Antoinette had previously been engaged to a colored relative, Sandi Cosway. After receiving the letter, Rochester spurns Antoinette. Using an obeah potion obtained from Christophine, Antoinette drugs and seduces Rochester. On waking, Rochester realizes that he has been drugged, and sleeps with Antoinette's maid in revenge. Betrayed, Antoinette seems to go mad herself. Part II ends with their departure from Granbois to Spanish Town, where Rochester plans to have Antoinette declared insane and confined.

Part III opens with Antoinette already confined in Thornfield Hall (in England), guarded by Grace Poole. Antoinette seems to have little sense of who or where she is at this point. Her stepbrother Richard Mason visits her, and she attacks him after he refuses to help her out of her marriage. Finally, she dreams that she escapes from her room and sets fire to the entire house. At the end of the dream, she flees to the top of the battlements, then jumps off. Antoinette wakes up, and the novel ends as she escapes from her room, with a candle lighting her way down a dark hallway.

## Part I, Section 1

### Subsection 1

- As the novel opens, we learn that Antoinette lives with her mother, Annette, and her brother, Pierre, on their dilapidated estate, Coulibri, outside Spanish Town, Jamaica. Antoinette's father, Mr. Cosway, passed away some time before. The local whites look down on them because Annette is from Martinique, a French colony. We also learn that, due to the recent passage of the Emancipation Act, their plantation, like many of the other plantations on the island, has fallen into disrepair because they can't, sniff, exploit slave labor anymore (for more historical context, see "Setting").
- Mr. Luttrell, a neighboring plantation owner who has also fallen on hard times, is so depressed that he shoots his dog and drowns himself in the ocean.
- Despite their poverty, Annette still enjoys getting dressed up and parading around on her horse even though she is mocked everywhere she rides. Antoinette finds her mother's horse – it has been poisoned. Annette accuses Godfrey, their servant, of knowing who poisoned the horse. Godfrey mumbles some stuff about the "devil prince" (I.1.1.10).
- A dead dog, a dead man, a dead horse…the body count in this novel is already getting

pretty impressive.

## Subsection 2

- Pierre has a mysterious disorder that impairs his ability to speak and to walk. Annette calls in a doctor. Although we're not told what he says, Annette is devastated. She avoids going out, and she barely talks to Antoinette. She spends much of her time wandering around the house talking to herself.
- Understandably freaked out by her mother's behavior, Antoinette hangs out with Christophine, who sings her melancholy songs in *patois* (http://www.merriam-webster.com/dictionary/patois). Antoinette doesn't understand all the words, but she does know that the songs are all about people being abandoned by their loved ones. (That's a pretty obvious piece of foreshadowing. In fact, everything that happens in Part I is a pretty obvious piece of foreshadowing…)

## Subsection 3

- Antoinette is chased by a girl who taunts her and calls her a "white cockroach," a derogatory term for white Creoles (see our discussion of "Race" in "Character Clues").
- Christophine discovers that the girl is Tia, the daughter of Christophine's friend Maillotte. Tia and Antoinette become friends.
- One morning, Antoinette drops some pennies that Christophine had given her. Tia bets Antoinette three pennies that Antoinette can't turn a somersault under water. Antoinette bets her all the pennies that she can.
- Antoinette turns one somersault underwater, starts to turn another one but can't complete it. Tia takes the money because she doesn't think Antoinette did a good somersault.
- Things get nasty as Antoinette calls Tia a "cheating nigger"; Tia fires right back and taunts Antoinette for being a "white nigger" (I.1.3.12-3).
- When Antoinette's back is turned, Tia disappears with Antoinette's dress. Antoinette puts on Tia's dress and heads home.
- When Antoinette arrives, she notices that two young women and a gentleman, all of whom are elegantly dressed, are visiting her mother. They laugh at her dress, and she runs away. Later, Christophine explains to Antoinette that these visitors are Luttrell's relatives, come to take over his plantation.
- When Antoinette goes to bed, she dreams that she is walking in a forest. Someone who hates her is stalking her. As she hears the stranger's footsteps coming closer, she fights and screams, but she's paralyzed.
- She wakes up crying. Her mother looks in on her, chides her for waking up her brother, and goes to check on Pierre.
- Antoinette thinks that Annette may have sold her last ring to buy them both new dresses. All of a sudden, Annette has become a social butterfly, spending every day with the Luttrells. For Antoinette, the house feels empty without her mother, so she spends most of her time outdoors.

### Subsection 4

- Antoinette is a bridesmaid at her mother's wedding to Mr. Mason in Spanish Town. She scowls at the wedding guests because she remembers over-hearing their malicious gossip about her family.

### Subsection 5

- Antoinette and Pierre stay with their aunt Cora in Spanish Town while Annette and Mr. Mason go off to Trinidad for their honeymoon.
- When Annette and Mr. Mason return, Antoinette admires her mother while she dances.
- Mr. Mason wonders why Aunt Cora didn't help them more when Mr. Cosway died. Antoinette explains that Aunt Cora's husband hated the West Indies, and Aunt Cora had to stay in England with her husband until he died.

### Subsection 6

- Mr. Mason, Annette, Antoinette, and Pierre return to Coulibri, which Mr. Mason has spruced up.
- Antoinette walks into Christophine's room and is fearful. Without seeing anything, she feels sure that an obeah charm is hidden somewhere in the room. We don't know if there is, in fact, a shriveled hand, some chicken feathers, and a nearly decapitated rooster piled somewhere in the room, because Christophine walks in cheerfully and Antoinette forgets the whole episode. Or thinks she does.
- After a year, Annette pushes Mr. Mason to take the family away from Coulibri. Annette insists that the blacks in the area (many of whom are her former slaves) are planning something terrible, but Mr. Mason thinks she's just paranoid. It's not clear why Mr. Mason wants to stick around so badly when he's got estates on other islands, but Antoinette is glad he wants to stay.

### Subsection 7

- On their way home after an outing, the family notices that the surrounding huts are empty. Mr. Mason wonders if there's a dance or a wedding. Annette is convinced that there's something more sinister going on and wants to leave the estate with Pierre.
- At dinner, Mr. Mason talks about his plan to import workers from the East Indies because he thinks the local population is too lazy. (Again, why does he want to stay?!) Annette warns him not to talk about his plans in front of Myra, their black servant, because she might tell the other blacks in the area of his plans.

- Antoinette peeks in on Pierre as he sleeps in his crib. She hears the bamboo creaking and a "sound like whispering" outside, but when she looks, she doesn't see anyone there (I.1.7.29). It's a full moon.
- Antoinette goes to bed, and waits for Christophine to come by to say good night – but there's no Christophine.
- Annette wakes Antoinette and tells her to get dressed. Antoinette hears her mother going next door to Pierre's room and talking with Myra, who's watching Pierre. Still half-asleep, Antoinette thinks she hears a chair fall in Pierre's room, and then gets up.

**Subsection 8**

- Everyone is assembled downstairs: Antoinette, Mr. Mason, Annette, Christophine (who has magically re-appeared without any explanation), and their servants, Mannie and Sass. Antoinette notices that both Godfrey and Myra are missing. Mr. Mason walks outside where a crowd has gathered. He asks them what they want, and he's greeted by a noise "like animals howling" (I.1.7.2).
- Annette wonders if it was a good idea to leave Pierre in his room alone with Myra (um…you think?). She wrings her hands, and her wedding ring falls off. Just then, Mannie notices that the back of the house where Pierre's bedroom is located is on fire.
- Annette runs to Pierre's bedroom and carries Pierre out in her arms. He seems lifeless, and his eyes have rolled back into his head. Annette berates Mr. Mason for refusing to leave Coulibri sooner. Mannie, Sass, and Christophine try to put out the fire.
- Everyone leaves the house through a back way. Mr. Mason tries to get Annette to leave, but she refuses abandon her parrot, Coco, a sad little bird who's been kind of snippy ever since Mr. Mason clipped his wings.
- Once outside, they find themselves taunted by a huge crowd. Antoinette doesn't recognize many of them, and wonders if they are not locals, but people who live by the bay.
- Mr. Mason curses at them, then decides to try a prayer. Just as he ends his prayer, the taunting stops.
- Was it the prayer? Maybe, maybe not. Because here comes Coco – that's right, the *parrot* . He's perched on a railing, his feathers on fire, but of course he can't escape because Mr. Mason clipped his wings. So the poor bird just sits there, flaming.
- Fortunately for everybody else, it's a common superstition that it's bad luck to kill a parrot or even watch a parrot die. So, before anyone can see Coco breathe his last, pitiful bird-breath, everyone looks away, and the rioters pull back.
- Antoinette and her family, however, aren't quite out of the woods yet. Their carriage is held up by a man who insists that they'll report the rioters to the police, who will return and punish the rioters all the more violently because they're black. Aunt Cora replies that the man will suffer all manner of torments in hell, which he seems to find compelling because he lets them into the carriage. A couple of women in the crowd seem to feel sorry for Antoinette and her family and begin to cry.
- But wait – Antoinette's not going in the carriage. She sees Tia and her mother in the distance, and runs to Tia. She sees Tia holding a jagged rock in her hand, but she doesn't see Tia throw it or feel the stone. Instead, she feels blood running down her face, and

when she looks up, Tia is also crying.

## Part I, Section 2

### Subsection 1

- Antoinette wakes up in a room in Aunt Cora's house. She's been ill for six weeks.
- Aunt Cora explains that they escaped to the Luttrells' home at Nelson's Rest, and from there rode to Aunt Cora's house. According to Aunt Cora, Pierre died on the way to Nelson's Rest, but Antoinette believes that Pierre died some time before that. Aunt Cora also claims that Annette is in the country recuperating, but Antoinette remembers hearing her mother scream at Mr. Mason and imitating Coco, screaming "*Qui est là? Qui est là?*" Aunt Cora sings Antoinette a few songs to help her sleep.

### Subsection 2

- Antoinette insists on visiting her mother with Christophine. Her mother is being cared for by a colored couple. When Antoinette goes to embrace her, her mother shoves her away.

### Subsection 3

- Antoinette steps out of Aunt Cora's house for her first day of school at Mount Calvary Convent.
- On the way, she is trailed by two children – a colored boy and a black girl. Both children harass her all the way to the convent gate. The girl shoves Antoinette, who drops her books.
- All of a sudden, another boy runs across the street to chase away the children. It's Sandi Cosway, a colored relative. (Interestingly, Antoinette doesn't remark on his race immediately as she does with other non-white characters.) After checking in on her, Sandi promises to keep the other children from harassing her.
- Antoinette finally enters the convent, where the nuns, who are of different races, comfort her, and Louise de Plana, another student, shows her around the school.

### Subsection 4

- Antoinette settles in to the routine at the school. She and the other students embroider while Mother St. Justine reads them stories about the lives of female saints, all of whom

rejected wealthy, handsome, eminently eligible suitors. Mother St. Justine also lectures them on the importance of hygiene, manners, and, of course, chastity. There's no dean's list at the school, but if there were, the de Plana sisters would be at the top.

- Antoinette feels compelled by those around her to forget her mother, or at least to think of her as dead. Without Christophine, who has left to live with her son, no one is around to speak of her mother, and Aunt Cora has decided to leave for England for her health.

## Subsection 5

- Antoinette gets into the routine of praying all the time – an awful lot of "Hail Mary's," if you're wondering about all that business about "now and at the hour of our death" – but soon starts questioning the point of all these prayers.
- She should be praying for eternal light for her mother, but she knows her mother hates bright light (and she's still alive, right?), so she stops praying for her mother.
- All the talk about ecstasy in heaven makes her eager to die, but then praying for death is a sin, so she prays not to pray for death. But then she wonders why so many things are sins, before she realizes that she's probably sinned again just by thinking that.
- If you're keeping count, she's praying not to think about thinking about why everything's a sin, including praying for death. Got it?
- Fortunately, Sister Marie Augustine steps in and explains that, as long as you chase away the sinful thought as soon as you think it, you haven't sinned. Antoinette gets so good at chasing away sinful thoughts that she doesn't feel compelled to pray anymore.
- While Antoinette works herself out of her religious conundrums, Mr. Mason has been visiting her frequently, taking her on little outings and giving her small gifts. After about eighteen months, he announces that it's time for her to leave the convent. He tells her he wants her to be "safe" and "secure," but these words do not inspire Antoinette with confidence. Instead, it fills her with soul-crushing fear. (Remember everything that happened at Coulibri, when Mr. Mason said everything was going to be all right and everyone should stop being paranoid?)
- Not surprisingly, Antoinette has her nightmare for the second time. Only this time there's a lot more detail. She's wearing a long, white dress (hint hint). Even though the stranger's face is "black with hatred," she doesn't try to escape (I.2.5.24). She follows him out of the forest into a garden and up some steps. She holds onto a tree, which sways as if it were trying to shake her loose.

## Subsection 6

- Sister Marie Augustine takes her out of the dormitory and offers her a cup of hot chocolate. Instead of comforting her, the chocolate reminds Antoinette of her mother's funeral.
- Mother's funeral, you ask? That's right – at some point last year, her mother died mysteriously, and Antoinette is just telling us now.
- Thinking of that sad moment, Antoinette asks Sister Marie Augustine why such terrible things happen, and Sister Marie Augustine replies that she doesn't know why "the devil

must have his little day" (I.2.6.9). Not exactly comforting. She tells Antoinette to go back to sleep.

# Part II, Section 1

## Subsection 1

- At this point, Rochester takes over the narrative. He and Antoinette arrive in the ominously named Massacre, on the nearby island of Dominica, for their honeymoon (for a discussion of the significance of the place, see "Setting"). He meets some of the servants, including Amélie, a saucy vixen who keeps giggling maliciously at him (or is he just being paranoid?). He thinks of how little he knows Antoinette. For most of the month before their marriage, he had been ill with a fever.
- The rain stops, and the porters carry the luggage on their heads. Amélie also carries some luggage on her head. A cock crows, and Rochester flashes back to their wedding night. They had slept in separate rooms because Antoinette was exhausted, and Rochester spent the night listening to the cocks' crowing. He remembers getting up early that morning and watching the women carry their trays to the kitchen on their heads, just as Amélie was.

## Subsection 2

- As the party approaches Granbois, Rochester is overwhelmed with the "wild" nature that surrounds him (II.1.2.1).
- In his head, he plans out a letter to his father which conveniently fills us in on the back-story. We find out that since he's not the first son, he inherits nothing from his father, so he has married Antoinette for her money.
- Upon arriving at Granbois, Rochester's not too impressed. Perhaps if he got over the whole English superiority thing he might be able to appreciate things more, but he can't. To him, everything looks like a sorry imitation of England – the dirt is red like England, the house looks like a rundown version of an English summer house. He does notice that for the first time Antoinette doesn't seem afraid or uneasy.
- The servants are waiting for them in front of the house – among them, Christophine. He doesn't find Christophine at all intimidating. Little does he know…
- Antoinette guides him into the house, where they clink a couple of glasses of rum and toast to happiness. She shows him around the place, and he continues to be less than enthusiastic.
- She shows him his dressing room, which used to belong to Mr. Mason. It's got a small bed, a desk, and a bookshelf with Byron's poetry, Sir Walter Scott's novels, and *Confessions of an Opium Eater*, among other things. (For the time period, 1839, these books are roughly equivalent to today's bestsellers, only a bit more highfalutin.) Baptiste

pops in and tells Rochester that Mr. Mason didn't like the place much.

- Rochester sits at the desk and finally writes out the letter to his father he's been thinking through in his head. The letter gives us a little more fill-in on the back-story. When he arrived in Spanish Town, he was down with a fever, and stayed with Mr. Fraser, a magistrate who loved to talk about his cases.
- Rochester wonders how the mail gets posted, and puts the letter back in his desk.

## Part II, Section 2

- Rochester flashes back to his courtship of Antoinette.
- It is unclear exactly how Rochester's marriage to Antoinette was arranged, but he arrived in Jamaica ready to play the part of a devoted suitor. He doesn't remember much of the wedding – he doesn't even remember what Antoinette looked like. He does remember the weird looks the guests gave him, but he's not sure exactly why they were acting so strangely.
- He then thinks back to the day before the wedding. Richard Mason informed him that Antoinette was unwilling to go through with the wedding. Rochester asked Antoinette why, and she said it was because she was afraid. Rochester did some smooth-talking to make her feel better, and the wedding was back on.

## Part II, Section 3

### Subsection 1

- Rochester thinks he may have fallen asleep during his flashbacks, because he hears Antoinette in the next room telling a woman not to put too much scent in her hair.

### Subsection 2

- At night, Rochester and Antoinette dine together. As for ambiance, they have plenty of it. The room is lit with candles, and the table is decked with beautiful pink flowers. Moths and beetles swarm the room, attracted by the light. As usual, Rochester is underwhelmed and finds dinner spicy.
- Antoinette asks Rochester if England is "like a dream," and Rochester replies that actually Jamaica is like a dream. They have a tiff over which is more "unreal."
- After dinner, they go outside. A giant moth flies into one of the candles, and Rochester saves it and lets it fly away.
- Antoinette tells Rochester about a time when she was at Granbois after…but she doesn't specify after what exactly. Rochester ignores her pause – he just doesn't want to hear any

depressing stories. (A little late for that, but let's move on.)

- Antoinette ignores Rochester and tells him that, one night, she woke to see two huge rats staring at her from a windowsill. She could see herself in the mirror looking at the rats, but she wasn't afraid. She fell asleep, and, when she woke again, she noticed that the rats had left and it's only then that she became afraid. She got up and slept outside in a hammock in the light of the full moon. Christophine was quite annoyed when she found Antoinette the next morning because it's bad luck to sleep under a full moon.
- Antoinette asks Rochester whether he thinks she's slept too much under a full moon. Instead of being freaked out, Rochester is touched by what he sees as her vulnerability. He embraces her while singing a soothing song about someone named Robin dying.
- They have a couple of glasses of wine and toast their happiness again.

## Subsection 3

- Rochester wakes up the next morning, feeling Antoinette watching him. Christophine waltzes in with some coffee, and tells Rochester to enjoy her wonderful coffee, which she describes as "bull's blood…not horse piss like the English madams drink" (II.3.3.4). Rochester is put off by Christophine's way of talking, but agrees.
- As Christophine walks slowly out of the room, her long dress trailing on the floor, Rochester asks Antoinette why Christophine isn't worried about her dress getting dirty. Antoinette explains that it's common custom to let your dress trail because it shows that you have other dresses. It is also a sign of respect on special occasions.
- Rochester also wonders why Christophine walks so slowly – to him, she seems lazy. Antoinette explains that Christophine isn't lazy, just methodical.
- Antoinette stretches out and tells him she's planning on spending the entire day in bed. She recommends that he check out the local swimming spots.

## Subsection 4

- Rochester and Antoinette often visit the bathing pool, a kind of small swimming pond.
- One day, a giant crab appears on a rock, and Antoinette throws a rock at it. Rochester asks her who taught her to throw so well, and she tells him that a boy named Sandi did.

## Subsection 5

- At night they watch the sunset from their summer home. Rochester notices that Antoinette is very generous to the servants, and he also notices that the servants' friends and families often visit, eating and drinking a lot, and Antoinette doesn't seem to notice.
- It is suggested that they haven't yet consummated their marriage, possibly because of Rochester's illness, but also because he still doesn't quite trust her.
- Rochester notices, however, that Antoinette seems to have let her guard down around him.

She's become more talkative, especially at night, when she talks about her sad childhood. She explains that before she met Rochester, she hadn't expected ever to be happy, but now that she is happy, she's afraid he'll take her happiness away from her. Rochester tells her that she doesn't have to be afraid around her.

- Finally, she asks, "If I could die. Now, when I am happy. Would you do that? You wouldn't have to kill me. Say die and I will die" (II.3.5.40).
- Rochester reads Antoinette's request as an invitation to get it on, so they finally have sex. A whole lot of it. All the time. But Rochester believes that it isn't love, just plain old physical lust.

# Part II, Section 4

## Subsection 1

- Amélie hands Rochester a letter from Daniel Cosway.
- The letter is somewhat hard to follow, as Daniel switches back and forth between wordy bouts of self-pity and gossip about Antoinette's family. Daniel's letter is basically another version of the events that we've learned so far from Antoinette. According to Daniel, however, the Cosways have brought their fate upon themselves through immoral behavior (randy Mr. Cosway) and the inherent madness that all white Creoles share. Daniel claims that Richard Mason tricked Rochester into marrying Antoinette, and implies that Christophine or some form of black magic was involved. Daniel also claims that he's too stupid to make up these stories, so they must be true.
- To confirm his story, Daniel tells Rochester to ask Richard Mason three questions: 1) whether Antoinette's mother was murderously insane; 2) whether Antoinette's brother was an "idiot"; 3) and whether Antoinette is also insane. He also asks Rochester to come visit him for more information – Amélie knows the way.
- After reading this letter, Rochester is stunned. He walks along the river, and, when he returns, he catches Amélie telling Antoinette that Christophine is leaving.
- When Amélie sees Rochester, she laughs and says he looks as if he's seen a zombie, and suggests that he's sick of Antoinette and plans on leaving her as well. Antoinette hits Amélie, Amélie hits back, and Rochester has to break up the fight. As Amélie leaves, she sings a mocking song about a "white cockroach."
- Christophine comes in and explains that she's leaving because she knows that Rochester doesn't like her, and she doesn't want to create friction between the two. She threatens Amélie with dire consequences if Amélie doesn't behave, and leaves, muttering some *patois*. Antoinette retreats into her room.

## Subsection 2

- Antoinette still hasn't left her room, so Rochester decides to take a nap. When he wakes

up, she seems to be asleep, so he decides to go for a walk.

## Subsection 3

- On his walk, Rochester gets lost in a dark forest. In many ways, this walk is like Antoinette's nightmare, only instead of being followed by a strange, hostile stranger, Rochester feels that the entire forest is "hostile." He follows what looks like an old paved road until he hits a clearing and the ruins of a stone house. At the bottom of a wild orange tree, he sees bunches of flowers tied with grass.
- A small girl sees Rochester. He tries to greet her, but she screams and runs away.
- Rochester tries to find his way back, but gets lost as night descends. Finally, Baptiste tracks him down and guides him back to the house.
- Antoinette still hasn't left her bed, so Rochester decides to spend the night with some quiet reading. He flips open to a chapter on obeah, where he reads that zombies are either dead people who seem to be alive or live people who seem to be dead. The author notes that blacks refuse to discuss obeah, or, when they do, they usually lie. The effects of obeah magic – or vodou, as it is called in Haiti – are attributed to an untraceable poison.

# Part II, Section 5

## Subsection 1

- Antoinette sets out on horseback to visit Christophine. At Mounes Mors (which means "the Dead Ones,") the horse stumbles, so Antoinette has to get off and walk the horse the rest of the way.
- Seeing Christophine, Antoinette flashes back to a childhood memory of Christophine washing her clothes by the river along with some women. She remembers feeling as if she belonged there.
- Antoinette tells Christophine that Rochester no longer loves her, and asks Christophine for her advice. At first, Christophine tells Antoinette to leave Rochester for a short while (i.e., play hard to get). She utters the time-honored wisdom that "when man don't love you, more you try, more he hate you, man like that" (II.5.1.14). Christophine suggests Antoinette go to Martinique, but Antoinette says she might go to England.
- At the thought of England, Antoinette has the uncanny feeling that, even though she's never been to England, she knows exactly what she'll find there: the look of snow, a bed with red curtains, and the end of her recurring nightmare. Christophine dismisses this idea.
- But really this is just Antoinette's way of warming up Christophine for her real request: she wants Christophine to fix her up an obeah potion. Christophine balks. At first she says it's just nonsense, as if she's denying that obeah exists, and then she says that "bad bad trouble come when *béké* meddle with that," which suggests that she believes that obeah works (II.5.1.37).

### Subsection 2

- Antoinette then has a flashback to an unspecified time before her wedding when she overheard her aunt Cora arguing with Richard Mason over the wedding arrangements. Aunt Cora believed it was scandalous for Richard to sign over Antoinette's inheritance to Rochester, but Richard insisted that Rochester was an honorable man.
- After the argument, Antoinette walked in, and Aunt Cora offered her a bag with her rings to sell just in case Antoinette needed the money.
- Antoinette must have sold one ring, as she says that she wants to sell "another" but isn't sure if she can find a buyer on this island.

### Subsection 3

- Christophine gives Antoinette the surprisingly good advice that Antoinette should just *talk* to the guy, coolly and rationally (not, say, in those weird, morbid nighttime conversations about unhappiness and death). But Antoinette is so distraught that, after drawing some random lines and circles in the dirt, Christophine agrees to give her a potion, but only if Antoinette agrees to talk to the guy first. Of course, if she's already given Antoinette the potion, then there's no way for her to take it back if Antoinette doesn't keep to the bargain, so...well, you know what's coming.
- Antoinette offers Christophine money, which Christophine rejects. However, it is unclear whether Christophine really does give back the money, because Antoinette later states that she had "forced" Christophine to make her a potion with her "ugly money" (II.5.3.30).
- As Antoinette leaves, she hears a cock crowing, which echoes back to all the other times that characters have heard cocks crowing. Only here, Antoinette thinks of Judas, making an explicit link to the Biblical story of treachery.

## Part II, Section 6

### Subsection 1

- While Antoinette visits Christophine, Rochester is back at the summer house. Amélie passes him a second letter from Daniel. In the first few lines, Daniel threatens to come over to the summer house and harass Rochester.
- Rochester asks Amélie for information about Daniel. The information she gives is somewhat contradictory. On the one hand, it seems as though Daniel had some training as a preacher, a "very superior man, always reading the Bible and...liv[ing] like white people." On the other hand, his parents are colored, although he told Rochester his father was white (Mr. Cosway), and he is, in Amélie's words, a "bad man."

- Amélie tells Rochester to go see Daniel; otherwise, Daniel probably will create a ruckus. She also adds that Daniel's brother, Alexander, is the well-to-do coloured father of Sandi Cosway, the boy who saved Antoinette in Part I, and that she thinks that Sandi and Antoinette were once engaged.
- Rochester thinks he hears Amélie say that she's sorry for him as she walks out of the room, but she denies it.

## Subsection 2

- Rochester visits Daniel Cosway, who has already started to hit the rum pretty hard.
- He tells Rochester about the time when he visited Mr. Cosway as a teenager, asking Mr. Cosway to acknowledge and support him financially. Mr. Cosway laughed in his face and said some terrible things about Daniel's mother. It is hard not to feel a little bad for Daniel because Mr. Cosway was a slave-owner who, it seems, was pretty unapologetic about sleeping with his female slaves and even less apologetic about supporting his children by those slaves.
- Daniel then delves into his family tree a bit, and tells Rochester about his half-brother, Alexander, and says he witnessed some intimate moment between Sandi Cosway and Antoinette. Daniel also claims that Christophine had to leave Jamaica after she was jailed for practicing obeah.
- (Oddly, even at the mention of obeah, Daniel can't seem to talk too explicitly about it – does he fear it, even though he's supposedly a Christian man? Is he fulfilling a racial stereotype?)
- Finally, Daniel gets to the point – he thinks Rochester, in the typical English way, wants to avoid scandal and he's willing to accept money to stay quiet about all he knows. Perhaps not the best move, because he just explained to Rochester that everyone, white and black, knows what he knows…
- Rochester rejects Daniel's blackmail and leaves, but not before Daniel taunts him with the supposed fact that Antoinette is related to his own despicable, "yellow" self.

## Subsection 3

- The scene opens as Antoinette tries to clear the air with Rochester. Rochester asks her why she claims her mother died just a short while ago when she had previously said that her mother had died when she was a child. Antoinette explains that "[t]here are always two deaths, the real one and the one people know about" (II.6.3.19).
- (Did that clear things up for you? Didn't think so.)
- Rochester then explains that he received a letter from Daniel. Antoinette denies that Daniel is related to her, and says that Daniel's real last name is Boyd, and he's got it in for all white people and for some reason really, really hates her. (The novel doesn't give us enough information to sort out who's right in this matter…)
- Rochester notices how exhausted Antoinette looks, and suggests that they talk during the day. Antoinette insists on clearing up the matter that night. Rochester relents.

- Rochester doesn't seem like such an ogre during this dialogue, even though he was resistant at first. Antoinette hesitates. To get her going, Rochester reminds her that she'd told him that her mother was miserable.
- Antoinette explains that it was a terrifying time for her mother after Mr. Cosway died. For a few years, they lived together on the dilapidated estate isolated from the rest of the world with no one to help except a few servants, including Christophine. After the incident with Antoinette's dress, "everything changed." Antoinette blames herself for all of her mother's efforts to find a husband to provide for their family, which ended up costing her mother her sanity and her brother his life.
- Antoinette explains that she believes her mother died the first death when Coulibri was destroyed, because her mother was so closely identified with the place.
- She then tells Rochester that, during one of her visits to her mother, she spied the man who was taking care of her mother – who at this point was clearly disoriented – feed her rum and embrace her. Antoinette strongly implies that she witnessed her mother's rape.
- Antoinette grows silent at this point, and laughs. Rochester hears her saying to herself that she has tried to talk to him, but "nothing has changed" (II.6.3.61).
- Calling her Bertha, Rochester asks her about her visit to Christophine. Antoinette says that Christophine told her to leave him. Rochester at this point suggest that he needs some time to process what Antoinette has told him, and suggests that they go to bed.
- As they go to bed, he notices a white powder on the floor. Antoinette says that it's to keep the cockroaches away.
- At this point, Rochester seems almost at the point of accepting Antoinette. "Why shouldn't we be happy?" he asks her. To the reader, he says, "She need not have done what she did to me. I will always swear that" (II.6.3.88). But the section ends with his speaking in a voice not his own, and remembering putting out the lights on the table before he blacks out.


## Subsection 4

- Rochester wakes from a dream where he is buried alive. He can't breathe, and realizes that Antoinette's heavy, perfumed hair has fallen across his mouth. He's dimly aware that he's been poisoned. He tastes the wine, and it's bitter.
- He runs out of the house, and finds himself back at the ruined old house where he'd seen the obeah offering. He falls asleep, and, when he gets up, he finds his way back to the summer house without getting lost this time.
- He hangs out in his dressing room, certain that Amélie is going to walk in and tell him that she feels sorry for him. Sure enough, Amélie walks in, feeds him some dinner as if he were a child, and voila, they sleep together.
- When he wakes up, he regrets what he's done, even though he feels great ("satisfied and peaceful"). He knows that Antoinette must have heard everything in the room next door, and when he looks at Amélie's sleeping face, he is repulsed by what he sees as her "darker" skin and "thicker" lips (84).
- When she wakes up, Amélie knows what's going on. After a brief, friendly conversation, Rochester offers her some money and they chat a little more about Amélie's plans to find a rich guy to marry in Rio.
- Rochester asks Amélie whether she's still sorry for him, and she is, but she says she'll try

to feel sorry for Antoinette as well.

- When Amélie closes the door, Rochester hears his wife leaving the house on horseback.

## Subsection 5

- After his little fling, Rochester takes another nap. When he wakes up, Baptiste informs him that the cook is leaving. Rochester notices that Baptiste doesn't seem quite as deferential as he used to be.
- Rochester writes a letter to Mr. Fraser, the magistrate in Spanish Town, asking for information on obeah on the pretext that he's writing a book on the topic, but really seeking information about Christophine.
- In his reply a few days later, Fraser writes that Christophine had indeed been imprisoned for practicing obeah, and that Mr. Cosway had befriended her and given her some property near Granbois. Fraser adds that he's letting the local police inspector know that Christophine is back in Rochester's neighborhood. If Christophine tries any of her funny business, Rochester can just call up the police inspector.

## Subsection 6

- We are not told exactly how many days have passed since Antoinette left Granbois, but we know that it's dusk when she finally returns. She heads straight to her room and demands some rum. Rochester also helps himself to some rum and goes to her room.
- When he opens the room, Antoinette looks a wreck: "her hair hung uncombed and dull into her eyes which were inflamed and staring, her face was very flushed and looked swollen" (II.6.6.18).
- Antoinette yells at his hypocrisy for sleeping with Amélie and paying her off as if he were just another slave owner taking advantage of one of his female slaves.
- She also yells at him for calling her "Bertha," arguing that the re-naming constitutes his own form of obeah, as a way of his trying to change her into someone else. According to Antoinette, Rochester has turned her beloved Granbois, the only place left to her where she loved and felt loved, into a place she hated.
- Things get ugly as Rochester tries to take the bottle away from her, and Antoinette bites into his arm. She breaks a bottle and threatens him with it, throwing obscenities at him all the while.
- Christophine intervenes at this point and tries to calm Antoinette down.
- Rochester leaves the room and bandages his arm. He feels as though the whole place is his enemy – even the telescope hates him. That has to hurt.
- He overhears Christophine cooing over Antoinette in *patois*, and Christophine's cooing makes him feel sleepy. He goes back into the larger room and decides he needs some more rum. Bad idea.

### Subsection 7

- Before Rochester can go to sleep, Christophine pops in and berates him for breaking Antoinette's heart. Rochester says that it is actually Christophine and her obeah which has made Antoinette into a total wreck.
- As Christophine really starts laying into Rochester, the novel takes a weird turn. Snippets of Christophine's diatribe are presented as echoing in Rochester's mind. It could be that the novel is trying to represent Rochester's state of mind – drunk, sleepy, barely able to respond to Christophine's attacks. Or is there perhaps a more sinister explanation – is Christophine's language actually paralyzing Rochester? Is she hexing him in some way, making him act zombie-esque? In this weird, trance-like dialogue, fragments pop up that couldn't possibly be Rochester's own thoughts, such as a bit of Antoinette's voice. Has Rochester gone telepathic all of a sudden? Or is it just the narrative being really clever?
- From this weird dialogue, it appears that during Rochester's fight with Antoinette (see previous subsection), Antoinette had confirmed all of Daniel's assertions, but Christophine claims that Antoinette only said these things to hurt Rochester. (We'll never know, because the novel doesn't give us "the truth" – just different perspectives. ARGH.)
- But Rochester snaps out of it once Christophine starts talking money. She offers to take Antoinette away if Rochester will leave her half her fortune. (Remember that bit where Richard Mason signed over all of Antoinette's fortune to Rochester?)
- Rochester isn't having any of it, and tells her he plans to get Antoinette medical attention. Christophine snaps back that it is in Rochester's best interest to have Antoinette declared mad and stuck in an asylum so that he can enjoy her fortune unencumbered.
- After more hectoring, Christophine mutters to herself, and Rochester knows it's not *patois*. (Then what is it? Again, the novel doesn't say.) Christophine finally leaves.

### Subsection 8

- Rochester is strangely energized from his battle with Christophine. No longer tired, he has another swig of rum and writes a letter to his father to let his father know that he plans on leaving Jamaica with Antoinette as quietly as possible.
- A cock crows. Rochester throws a book at it. It hops aside and crows some more. Baptiste claims that it is crowing for a change of weather, but we know from the previous times that a cock has crowed that a betrayal is being signaled.
- Rochester idly draws a three-storied, English-style house with a stick-figure woman in a room on the top floor, a not-so-subtle allegory of what he plans on doing to Antoinette when they're back in England.

## Part II, Section 7

- Rochester has a contemplative moment on a cloudy summer day that's more reminiscent of an English summer than a Caribbean one. He mentions that it's almost hurricane

season, which runs from August to October.

- His thoughts reflect his conflicting feelings toward Antoinette. He starts by thinking of how much he hates her, how she'll cheat on him with anyone and everyone, how crazy he thinks she is, and how he'll make sure that she loves and is loved by no one. He plans to break her just as a hurricane wind blasts a tree.
- Then his thoughts take a sentimental turn. If only her "blank hating moonstruck face" would show some emotion, if only she would shed a tear, he would embrace and console her – as long as her emotion is presented to him, for him alone to enjoy. He calls her his "mad girl" (II.7.18).
- The subsection ends with his noting that the weather has changed, a reference back to the cock crowing in the previous section.

## Part II, Section 8

- Antoinette, Rochester, and their porters are getting ready to leave Granbois. Baptiste says good-bye, scarcely concealing his contempt for Rochester.
- Rochester is surprised by his own sadness on leaving Granbois. Regret, maybe? On an impulse, he apologizes to Antoinette, who only looks back at him blankly. This doesn't surprise Rochester, but that pretty much does it for his apologetic mood.
- At this point, Antoinette is more than just indifferent – she seems petrified. Rochester can't stop talking about her doll-like expression, the stiffness of her movements. (Of course, it's partly his fault because he keeps calling her a "marionette," and then there was that thing he did with her maid…)
- Antoinette's state reminds Rochester again of how alien his surroundings are to him, and how he has always felt that the surroundings concealed a secret. He compares this secret to a treasure sunk deep in the sea. Since the law says that finders can only keep a third, many treasure-seekers don't tell anybody when they've located a treasure, preferring to sell their treasure in some clandestine way. He feels the same way about Antoinette and has the random thought that they should be like pirates who keep all their treasure for themselves. And who doesn't like a good pirate adventure?
- Rochester, that's who. Instead of that promising avenue, Rochester sees Antoinette's hating stare, and can't help hating her back.
- Rochester's musings are interrupted by a wailing servant boy. Antoinette explains that she'd promised the boy that he could join them because the boy liked Rochester so much. (Random, isn't it?) Rochester berates Antoinette for making promises in his name.
- Part II ends with the boy trailing after them holding a basket on his head, still crying.

## Part III, Section 1

- Part III opens from Grace Poole's point of view. By this point, Antoinette has been locked up in an attic in Thornfield Hall, Rochester's estate in England. Grace has been hired to guard and nurse Antoinette.

- In this brief section, Grace talks to Leah, a fellow servant, about how she ended up working at Thornfield. When Grace had gone in for a job interview with Mrs. Eff (short for Mrs. Fairfax), Mrs. Eff had insisted that no gossip was permitted, and Rochester was willing to pay her handsomely to keep quiet. Mrs. Eff had also told Grace that Rochester was no monster, but a decent man who'd obviously experienced some incredible tragedy.
- Grace agrees to Mrs. Eff's terms, even though she believes that there already numerous rumors about Rochester and his wife in the village. She remembers meeting Antoinette and noting how frail and thin Antoinette looked.
- She thinks to herself that the manor is a safe haven from all the rumors in the world, and perhaps that's why she, Mrs. Eff, and Leah are drawn to its isolation.

## Part III, Section 2

- We're back in Antoinette's head now. Antoinette doesn't remember how or why she ended up in the room – she's just really, really cold.
- She thinks that if she only saw "him" (in this section as in all the others, Rochester is never named), she could persuade him to let her go, but she hasn't seen him since she's been locked up in the room.
- She's aware that a woman named Mrs. Poole sleeps in her room. She watches Mrs. Poole count the money from a money bag tied around her neck, then get drunk and fall asleep.
- She tries whatever Mrs. Poole is drinking – it's clear and tastes nothing like rum, but she feels that she can think and remember more clearly after she's had a taste.

## Part III, Section 3

- In Antoinette's room, there is a high window and an open bed. Next to a small dressing room is another room hung with tapestries. Antoinette thinks she sees an image in one of the tapestries of her mother dressed in an evening gown with bare feet.
- There's no mirror, so Antoinette doesn't know what she looks like. She's not sure who or where she is.
- Through the tapestry room is a passageway, where Antoinette spies Mrs. Poole whispering with Leah. Although the room is kept locked up, Antoinette knows where Mrs. Poole hides the keys.
- When Mrs. Poole is asleep, Antoinette steals the keys and slips out into the passage. However, she doesn't think she's in a real house, but a cardboard one. She has heard that she's in England, but she doesn't believe it.
- She remembers being on board a ship to England. She tried to get a young man who brought her food to help her, but Rochester caught her. She was drugged to sleep and, when she awoke, she noticed that the sea was different. But she still doesn't believe she's in England – just a cardboard world.

## Part III, Section 4

- When Antoinette wakes up, she notices that her wrists have red marks on them and doesn't know why.
- Mrs. Poole tells her that a gentleman had come to visit her the day before, but Antoinette doesn't remember anything. She thinks there are visitors in the house, and she does remember seeing a woman during her night-time ramblings through the house. The woman was frightened and found another woman, who explained that she'd seen a ghost.
- Mrs. Poole explains that the gentleman was her brother, Richard Mason, and when he came to visit her, Antoinette had attacked him with a knife.
- Mrs. Poole says that she won't do anything to help Antoinette anymore. She'd convinced Mrs. Eff to let Antoinette go outside to get some fresh air, but while Mrs. Poole napped under a tree, Antoinette must have bought a knife from a passing stranger. Antoinette remembers trading her locket with a woman.
- Mrs. Poole also reminds Antoinette that her brother, Richard Mason, had said that he could not intercede "legally" in Antoinette's marriage, and it was then that Antoinette had stabbed him.
- Antoinette then remembers the incident, and remembers how Richard didn't seem to recognize her at first. She asks Mrs. Poole if she was wearing her red dress; Mrs. Poole says "no." Antoinette thinks that if she'd worn her red dress, her brother would have recognized her.

## Part III, Section 5

- The red dress reminds Antoinette of the last time she saw Sandi Cosway in Spanish Town. She was wearing the red dress when Sandi had asked her to run away with him. She refused.
- Apparently they had an affair when Rochester was away. Their last kiss is described as a "life and death kiss," and she remembers hearing a white ship whistling as they kissed.

## Part III, Section 6

- Antoinette holds the red dress against herself and asks Mrs. Poole if it makes her look "unchaste," as Rochester said it did. Mrs. Poole tells her to put it away and warm herself with a grey shawl.
- Antoinette drops the dress on the floor and compares it to a fire spreading across the room. The dress reminds her that there is something she must do, but she can't remember what.

## Part III, Section 7

- Antoinette has her dream for the third and last time, only this time she knows how it ends.
- In her dream, she steals Mrs. Poole's keys and lets herself out of the room. The house seems empty, the guests are gone, and the bedrooms locked up. But she still feels as if someone is chasing her and laughing at her.
- She finds herself in a room with a red carpet and red curtains, but everything else in the room is white. She thinks she must be in some kind of chapel, but she can't find an altar, only a gold clock.
- Antoinette sits on a soft couch, and feels incredibly drowsy. All of a sudden, she is transported back to Aunt Cora's room. She sees the sunlight coming in, and the tree outside casts its shadow on the floor. But the sight of the candles transports her back to the red room. She knocks all the candles down – one of them sets fire to the curtains, and Antoinette enjoys the spectacle.
- Antoinette goes back into the hallway and sees what she thinks is the ghost the other women were speaking of. Frightened, she drops her candle and sets fire to the tablecloth.
- As she runs away or flies, she calls on Christophine to help her. She believes Christophine sends her a wall of fire to protect her from the ghost, but the wall of fire is too hot for her, so she runs away up the stairs.
- She passes her own room up to the battlements on the roof of the house. She hears shouting, but ignores it. Sitting on top of the battlements, she sees a red sky with her entire life depicted in it. The sky is filled with images of life in Coulibri and Granbois.
- She thinks she hears Coco calling "*Qui est là? Qui est là?*" and Rochester calling her "Bertha! Bertha!"
- She leans over, and sees the pool at Coulibri. Tia is in the pool beckoning to her, and when Antoinette doesn't jump, Tia laughs at her. Antoinette hears screaming, and wonders why she is screaming. She calls out to Tia, jumps – then wakes up.
- Mrs. Poole hears Antoinette scream and checks in on her, but Antoinette pretends to be asleep. Mrs. Poole goes to bed. When Antoinette hears her snore, she gets up and unlocks the door.
- "Now at last I know why I was brought here and what I have to do," Antoinette says. She shields a candle in the palm of her hand as she walks down the "dark passage" (III.7.6).

## Themes

## Theme of Race

Race is absolutely integral to the way that the characters understand themselves and their place in society. Some writers and scholars claim that Rhys's *Wide Sargasso Sea* portrays black characters as flat stereotypes – child-like, primitive, animalistic. But what if we were to give the novel the benefit of the doubt? That's not to say we should excuse the language. Instead, we might consider how everything is told from a *character's* point of view, and not necessarily the *author's* . It could be that these characters' *expectations* about race are tested by the novel itself, particularly with a Creole character such as Antoinette, who alternately identifies with both

white and black communities. (See our discussion of "Race" in "Character Clues" for a rundown of racial categories operating at the time of the novel.)

## Questions About Race

1. What are the different characters' attitudes toward race? How do these attitudes affect the way they perceive themselves and relate to other people?
2. How are different races depicted in the novel? Do you find that the black characters are less complex or sympathetic than the white or Creole characters, or vice versa? Why?
3. How do issues of class and gender complicate the issue of race in the novel? For example, how does the situation of a black female character such as Amélie exhibit similarities or differences with the situation of a Creole female character such as Antoinette?

## Chew on Race

While Antoinette is often critical of Rochester for his hypocritical attitude toward racial equality, Antoinette does not recognize the extent of her own racial prejudices.

Black characters in the novel seem to lack depth or voice only because they are presented through the eyes of white or Creole characters; the novel presents black characters in this way to show how racial stereotypes contribute to the representation of non-white characters.

## Theme of Identity

While Antoinette's constant questioning of who she is takes center stage, many of the other characters in *Wide Sargasso Sea* also struggle to make sense of their identities during the tumultuous historical period described in the novel. Characters must navigate challenges to the ways that race, gender, and class affect their identities. Their mental states are often altered due to illness, alcohol, narcotics, or even obeah. Often, other characters serve as mirrors or doubles who reveal unexpected desires and commonalities, as Tia does for Antoinette.

## Questions About Identity

1. How do race, class, gender, and culture affect the characters' identities and their attitudes toward each other?
2. What specific events bring on identity crises for different characters? How do they respond to these crises? Do you think they come out of these crises with a stronger sense of who they are, or do you think these crises leave the characters shattered and powerless?
3. How do the characters' relationships affect their sense of who they are? How do friendships, family relations, relationships between masters and servants, and romantic relationships empower or destroy the characters?

## Chew on Identity

Ironically, Antoinette's relationships with the people closest to her in terms of race and class contribute to her breakdown; it is only in her relationships with characters from other races and classes – such as Tia and Christophine – that she feels most comfortable with herself.

In showing how Rochester unwittingly mimics Caribbean cultural practices, such as the practice of obeah, the novel demonstrates that his effort to distinguish Caribbean characters as essentially alien and different from himself is futile.

## Theme of Language and Communication

Language in *Wide Sargasso Sea* isn't just a medium for communicating thoughts and feelings, but a social force that actually shapes the fates of the characters. It marks a character's place in society, as when the black characters use a dialect of English that sounds broken or even obscene to the white characters. It can signal the introduction of a foreign or exotic element, as when Christophine speaks in *patois*, a dialect of French spoken in the Caribbean. In the form of gossip or lies, language can inspire as much fear and distrust as an actual threat, and it can manufacture scandals that ruin people's lives. As a product of language itself, the novel wrestles with the medium, drawing attention to the ways in which stories are told and received.

## Questions About Language and Communication

1. How is the history of Antoinette's childhood and family told by different characters? How does Antoinette's version contrast with Daniel's, for example, or Christophine's? How do rumors – what the unnamed "they" say in Part I, for example – represent Antoinette's family history?
2. What are some successful and unsuccessful instances of communication in the book? Compare and contrast the dialogues between Annette and Mr. Mason, Antoinette and Rochester, and Christophine and Rochester, among others.
3. How is language an actual force in the book? Consider, for example, how Christophine's power depends on what people *say* she can do, or how powerful simply applying a label on a person – such as "mad" – can be.
4. Rochester talks a lot about the "secret" of the island and the "secret" Antoinette can't tell. What do you think the secret is? How does this secret relate to the project of the book as a whole to tell the untold story of *Jane Eyre*'s "madwoman in the attic"?

## Chew on Language and Communication

Antoinette's tragic view of life and her deep suspicion of Rochester leads her to reject an open dialogue with him about her past, and with it the possibility of a genuine relationship.

By leaving open the question of whether Christophine's obeah actually works, the novel focuses attention on how much rumor, or the mythology that the community has constructed around obeah, contributes to obeah's so-called "magical" power.

## Theme of Love

You're more likely to see the theme of love treated in *Wide Sargasso Sea* under one of its many associated emotions: desire, lust, trust, and happiness, but also hate, fear, and jealousy. Romantic love in the novel is constantly thwarted by all the baggage the characters bring into their relationship, including their past histories and their ideas about race, gender, and class. Antoinette is not necessarily exempt from the same kind of racism that marks Rochester's attitude toward herself and Amélie, as her relationship with Sandi Cosway shows. (For a longer discussion of death as a metaphor for sexuality, see "Mortality.")

## Questions About Love

1. Think about Annette's experiences and Antoinette's religious education. How do they affect Antoinette's attitude toward romantic love?
2. How do different characters perceive the relationship between sexual desire and love? Between love and happiness?
3. How do male and female characters differ on issues of love, marriage, and sex? In addition to Antoinette and Rochester, you might also want to look at Christophine, Amélie, Aunt Cora, Richard Mason, and Daniel.
4. What do Antoinette's and Rochester's sexual or romantic relationships with other characters tell us about their attitudes toward love? Consider, for example, Antoinette's relationship with Sandi Cosway or Rochester's with Amélie.

## Chew on Love

For Rochester, neither Antoinette nor Amélie are worthy of romantic love because of their racial status; instead, they are objects to be owned and enjoyed sexually.

In the novel, marriage is often a financial transaction that deprives women of economic and political power; only women who can work outside marital boundaries such as Christophine, Amélie, and Aunt Cora can assert some control over their own lives.

## Theme of Mortality

While there are certainly many deaths in *Wide Sargasso Sea* (Antoinette's entire family, for example), neither Antoinette nor Rochester actually die. Instead, death for them becomes a potent metaphor for all of the ways in which selves can be lost, transformed, or destroyed. The novel plays on the literary tradition of equating death with orgasm in order to suggest how sex between the characters can be a form of control, rather than pleasure. The novel is also littered with people who act like zombies, beings that are both alive and dead, and ghosts, beings that are neither alive nor dead.

## Questions About Mortality

1. What are the different ways of dying in the novel? Consider, for example, death as a metaphor for sex, death as social death or a retreat from society, death as a loss of sanity,

and death as a loss of identity.

2. What are some specific instances where characters act as if they were dead, as zombies or ghosts? What does this death-like state say about their situation or their state of mind?

3. How can death be understood not as the loss of a self, but as a necessary step toward the development of a new understanding of the self? For example, consider different ways of reading Antoinette's last dream at the end of the novel.

## Chew on Mortality

In *Wide Sargasso Sea*, zombies, or the living dead, are used to symbolize the different ways that characters can be physically alive but socially or emotionally dead at the same time.

Antoinette's dream of committing suicide at the end of *Wide Sargasso Sea* actually signifies her rejection of her racial prejudices and her ultimate identification with the black Caribbean community.

## Theme of The Supernatural

Obeah (called "vodou" or "voodoo" in the French-speaking Caribbean), a folk religion indigenous to the Caribbean, casts a huge shadow over this novel, though whether its magic really works is up for debate. (Read more about obeah here). Obeah seems to inspire fear more through what it's rumored to do rather than through actual feats of magic. The Haitian revolution in 1791 was thought to be initiated by a voodoo ceremony, and obeah practitioners were imprisoned because they were thought to encourage slave insurrections (Rhys 1999: 75). In *Wide Sargasso Sea*, obeah is often juxtaposed to Christian beliefs and to rational, scientific thought, bringing up questions about how different systems of belief operate.

## Questions About The Supernatural

1. How are obeah and the practice of religion, specifically Christianity, similar? Consider, for example, the use of prayers and incantations, the importance of relics or holy/magical objects, and the figure of female practitioners, such as Christophine and Sister Marie Augustine.

2. Do you think Christophine's magic actually "works" in the world of the novel? If not, why do you think everybody is so terrified of Christophine? How does Christophine exert her influence over other people?

3. How do magical elements contribute to the novel's representation of life in the Caribbean?

## Chew on The Supernatural

In the novel, neither obeah nor Christianity are shown to be a superior way of understanding the world; both are shown to be belief systems that require the radical suspension of critical thought on the part of the individual.

The novel demystifies the magic of obeah by showing how it is a culturally specific expression of a community's identity and history.

## Theme of Power

*Wide Sargasso Sea* investigates the theme of power by looking at such institutions as marriage, empire, and slavery. These institutions are all ways in which a person or a group of people can dominate others. For Antoinette and her mother, marriage is a legal arrangement that results in the loss of their economic freedom. Through characters such as Mr. Mason and the Luttrells, the novel shows how the island colonies provided a rich source of income to England, the seat of imperial power. And racial relations continue to register the effects of slavery, even after it is officially ended in 1833, as the hostility of the Cosways' former slaves attest.

## Questions About Power

1. How does the novel register the consequences of the Emancipation Act of 1833? Have racial relations improved after the abolition of slavery, or do racial hostilities persist? What are some of the causes of persistent racial antagonism?
2. How are the characters affected by the legal ramifications of marriage in the novel? In what ways does marriage serve the needs of a patriarchal society?
3. How are the economic, social, and political structures of colonial Jamaica described in the novel? Can certain relationships between the characters be viewed as allegories for the exploitative system of imperialism? If so, how?
4. Given the systems of social, economic, and political oppression described in the novel, how do characters express their resistance to these systems? Do you think their resistance is effective?

## Chew on Power

Rochester uses the rhetoric of chastity, legality, and sanity to justify his control over Antoinette and her fortune.

What appears to the white characters as mere laziness or irrational, destructive behavior is actually an expression of protest on the part of the black Caribbean community against continuing economic and political injustices.

## Theme of Versions of Reality

As you read *Wide Sargasso Sea*, you might catch yourself asking, "OK, would somebody *please* tell me what's really going on here?" And you wouldn't be alone. In a novel that's written in such a deceptively simple style, all we get are different versions of events, and never what *really* happened. Without an objective, omniscient narrator telling us what's going on, the novel invites us to question the distinction between dream and reality, madness and sanity, superstition and reason, truth and falsity. By giving us a patchwork of different, equally compelling perspectives, the novel casts suspicion on anyone who would dare dismiss any one of those perspectives as less valid than the others.

## Questions About Versions of Reality

1. The novel never gives us an objective point of view, just the events as told through various characters. How does withholding the "truth" of what happened affect the way we read the novel? Is it possible that there's any "truth" to be found?
2. How does the novel differentiate between Antoinette's and Rochester's ways of looking at the world? How are they similar? Is Antoinette in fact mad, and Rochester sane and rational?
3. What is the relationship between Antoinette's recurring nightmares and the rest of the novel? Do dreams offer her a way to process particularly troubling events? Do they reveal hidden wishes or desires? Are they actual glimpses of the future? Or are they something else entirely? If they're only dreams, why are dream elements popping up in Rochester's reality?

## Chew on Versions of Reality

Antoinette's psychological instability is not due to racial or genetic factors, as Rochester believes, but precipitated by the numerous traumatic experiences that have shattered her sense of self.

By presenting not only different narratives, but also different representations of the same story through dreams, letters, and rumors, the novel calls attention to the different ways in which fictions contribute to our understanding of reality.

## Theme of Contrasting Regions

England and the Caribbean are constantly opposed in *Wide Sargasso Sea*, but what's more important is to think of England and the Caribbean are *ideas*, products of the imagination. England is just as much an exotic fiction to Antoinette and Christophine as the Caribbean is to Rochester. By exoticizing England in this way, the novel is overturning a long tradition of looking at non-European countries as other, alien, uncivilized – and thus ripe for colonial conquest, as seen in Rochester's constant attempt to get at the "secret" of the locale. Instead of being a far-off, foreign locale, the Caribbean becomes a place that reflects back on the characters' own notions of Englishness – you could say that one set of islands is a reflection of the other.

## Questions About Contrasting Regions

1. What aspects of England and the Caribbean are described in the novel? What aspects seem to be familiar and welcoming, and what aspects seem to be exotic or hostile?
2. How do the representations of each region reflect the characters' firsthand experience with the region, as opposed to what they may have learned through hearsay or through texts?
3. Do any of the characters ever feel completely at home in the Caribbean? Why or why not? What do their feelings say about their relationship to Caribbean society and culture in general? And to England and English society and culture?

## Chew on Contrasting Regions

Antoinette's experience of homelessness in both England and the Caribbean indicates how she is doubly at a disadvantage in both societies as a Creole and as a woman.

By reducing England to a cardboard box and accentuating the brilliant natural landscape of the Caribbean, Rhys overturns an English literary tradition of viewing the Caribbean as an exotic world home to everything foreign and hostile to English civilization, and indeed, to civilization in general.

## Race Quotes

*I never looked at any strange negro. They hated us. They called us white cockroaches. Let sleeping dogs lie. One day a little girl followed me singing, "Go away white cockroach, go away, go away." (I.1.3.2)*

Thought: Here Antoinette describes the hostility she encountered from blacks after the Emancipation Act was passed. With the death of her father, the former slave owner Mr. Cosway, her family is not only ruined, but exposed to the open threats and abuse of the area's black community, as the little girl's use of the term "white cockroach" indicates.

*Then Tia would light a fire (fires always lit for her, sharp stones did not hurt her bare feet, I never saw her cry). (I.1.3.3)*

Thought: Ironically, the same taunting girl in Quote #1 above is Tia, who becomes Antoinette's only friend. Antoinette strongly identifies with Tia because both are in racial groupings that are considered inferior to the dominant white, European colonial class. But this identification has a flip side: Tia is depicted here as having a closer connection to the natural world that Antoinette thinks of as a haven. Tia's close connection to the natural world is actually playing on a racial stereotype that views blacks as being primitive, as closer to nature than to civilized man.

*"They invent stories about you, and lies about me. They try to find out what we eat every day."*

*"They are curious. It's natural enough. You have lived alone far too long, Annette. You imagine enmity which doesn't exist. Always one extreme or the other. Didn't you fly at me like a little wild cat when I said nigger. Not nigger, nor even negro. Black people I must say."*

*"You don't like, or even recognize the good in them," she said, "and you won't believe in the other side."*

*"They're too damn lazy to be dangerous," said Mr. Mason. "I know that."*

*"They are more alive than you are, lazy or not, and they can be dangerous and cruel for reasons you wouldn't understand." (I.1.6.9-12)*

Thought: In this tiff, it appears that Annette and Mr. Mason are just throwing around some racial stereotypes. Annette thinks blacks are malicious, and Mr. Mason believes them to be lazy. Or you could read it another way. Annette could be disputing Mr. Mason's condescending belief that blacks are "lazy," incapable of action. Instead of this one-sided view, Annette is trying to get Mr. Mason to see that blacks are actual human beings, psychologically complex and fully capable of acting on their own desires.

*"What is all this," [Mr. Mason] shouted. "What do you want?" A horrible noise swelled up, like animals howling, but worse. (I.1.8.2)*

Thought: At this point, the novel seems to be agreeing with Mr. Mason's stereotypical view of blacks as primitive and animalistic. But remember that this is from Antoinette's point of view – she's telling the story. And a page or two later, Antoinette notices that some of the women rioters are crying in sympathy with her family's fate, so the rioters aren't all feral "howling." At the very least, the depiction of blacks at this point reflects Antoinette's conflicting feelings about race.

*[Amélie's] expression was so full of delighted malice, so intelligent, above all so intimate that I felt ashamed and looked away. (II.1.1.24)*

Thought: This quote is one of many in which Rochester reveals his almost paranoid concern with the way blacks perceive him. Since Amélie's expression is filtered through Rochester's narrative, it's hard to read her expression without thinking about what it reveals about Rochester's own feelings. Is he paranoid? Or is she really giving him this look? Does the fact that the look is "intimate" and causes Rochester to feel "ashamed" actually reveal more about Rochester's attraction to Amélie, an attraction that he can't admit to himself at this point but will, we know, act on later on in the novel?

*"Her coffee is delicious but her language is horrible and she might hold her dress up. It must get very dirty, yards of it trailing on the floor."*

*"When they don't hold their dress up it's for respect," said Antoinette. "Or for feast days or going to Mass."*

*"And is this a feast day?"*

*"She wanted it to be a feast day."*

*"Whatever the reason it is not a clean habit [...] And she looks so lazy. She dawdles about."*

*"Again, you are mistaken. She seems slow, but every move she makes is right so it's quick in the end." (II.3.3.5-14)*

Thought: Like Mr. Mason in Quote #2, Rochester expresses here a similar belief that blacks are lazy. Like her mother Annette, Antoinette is being placed in the position here of a guide or an interpreter, as somebody who can read the true significance of what blacks say and do. Of course, like her mother, Antoinette is ignored.

*This young Mrs. Cosway is worthless and spoilt, she can't lift a hand for herself and soon the madness that is in her, and in all these white Creoles, come out [...] Sir ask yourself how I can make up this story and for what reason [...] The good man in Barbados teach me more, he give me books, he tell me read the Bible every day and I pick up knowledge without effort. He is surprise how quick I am. Still I remain an ignorant man and I do not make up this story. I cannot. It is true. (II.4.1.9-17)*

Thought: This quote is representative of Daniel Cosway/Boyd's bizarre and contradictory letter. First off, he spouts a lot of racist baloney about Creoles that was unfortunately common belief at the time – the belief that they are somehow "degenerate" because of their exposure to the Caribbean climate. But then he tries to pump himself up. He's no ordinary colored, but an educated one, such that whites are astonished at how "quick" or clever he is. But he knows that if he pumps himself up too much, Rochester will just think he's fibbing, so he actually pins a racist stereotype on himself. As a colored man, he can't possibly be smart enough to make up a story, can he?

*"If béké say it foolishness, then it foolishness. Béké clever like the devil. More clever than God. Ain't so? Now listen and I will tell you what to do" (II.5.2.24)*

Thought: Christophine here expresses a canny sense of how her world works. Since the *békés* (or whites) hold political power, they are able to, in some sense, control what counts as reality. (The back-story here is that Christophine was sentenced to prison by a white magistrate for practicing obeah.) On the other hand, if the *békés don't* "say it foolishness," i.e., if they *do* believe in obeah, then obeah works, at least to the extent that an obeah practitioner like Christophine can frighten people into giving her what she wants (of which there are numerous examples throughout the book). Thus, even though she starts by admitting the power of the *béké*'s word, she ends the quote by *telling* Antoinette, a *béké*, what to do.

*But how can she know the best thing for me to do, this ignorant, obstinate, old negro woman, who is not certain if there is such a place as England? (II.5.1.32)*

Thought: It's difficult to be completely sympathetic with Antoinette when we see her racism in a moment such as this one. Despite her obvious sympathy and identification with the blacks in her world, she still maintains many racist attitudes, a possible contributing factor in her rejection of Sandi Cosway.

*For a moment Antoinette looked very much like Amélie. Perhaps they are related, I thought. It's possible, it's even probably in this damned place. (II.6.3.10)*

Thought: Here, Rochester is so convinced of Antoinette's status as racially inferior to him that everything he sees confirms what he already believes. Like the scene with Amélie's "intimate" gaze, Rochester reads a physical similarity between Amélie and Antoinette that justifies his treatment of them. That he can have sex with them without calling it "love" is supported by the fact that both relationships involve financial transactions: he gives money to Amélie, but receives money (as dowry) from Antoinette. No wonder Amélie says that she will try to feel sympathy for Antoinette – you could say Antoinette gets the short end of the stick.

## Identity Quotes

*I went to parts of Coulibri that I had not seen, where there was no road, no path, no track. And if the razor grass cut my legs and arms I would think, 'It's better than people.' Black ants or red ones, tall nests swarming with white ants, rain that soaked me to the skin – once I saw a snake. All better than people.*

*Better. Better than people.*

*Watching the red and yellow flowers in the sun thinking of nothing, it was as if a door opened and I was somewhere else, something else. Not myself any longer. (I.1.3.38)*

Thought: The wild beauty of the Coulibri estate provides the young Antoinette an escape from her troubles. But this estate isn't a home, a safe and secure place that Antoinette can identify with and make her own. The razor grass's mutilation of Antoinette's body marks a wound where her sense of self should be. Antoinette forgets her troubles to the point where she doesn't exist anymore, perhaps to the point where she isn't even human anymore, and that's not necessarily a good thing.

*We stared at each other, blood on my face, tears on hers. It was as if I saw myself. Like in a looking-glass. (I.1.8.29)*

Thought: Oh, boy, Antoinette gets cut *again*. This time by a rock thrown by Tia, although she never sees Tia actually throw the rock. Like the razor grass in Quote #1, Tia is an avatar of the unwelcoming home. Tia is an image of what Antoinette would like to be: a black woman, not a white Creole who is accepted by neither white nor black communities. Unlike Tia, Antoinette will never have a racial identity to call her own.

*I will write my name in fire red, Antoinette Mason, née Cosway, Mount Calvary Convent, Spanish Town, Jamaica, 1839. (I.2.4.1)*

Thought: Other than the fact that this is the only instance where we get an actual date in the novel, the quote is also interesting because it's a rare instance where Antoinette seems to embrace her identity. The fact that she has two last names (since her mother's re-marriage), yet another indication of her split identity, doesn't seem to faze her as she emblazons her signature in "fire red," a color that resonates with the moments where she is the most defiant in the novel (See "Red Dress, White Dress" in "Symbols, Imagery, Allegory"). This uncharacteristic confidence might have something to do with the fact that she feels the convent is a kind of "refuge," a community of racially diverse women, away from the grasp of marriage-minded, gold-digging, white English bachelors (I.2.5.1).

*It was a song about a white cockroach. That's me. That's what they call all of us who were here before their own people in Africa sold them to the slave traders. And I've heard English women call us white niggers. So between you I often wonder who I am and where is my country and where do I belong and why was I ever born at all. (II.4.1.61)*

Thought: In explaining her conflicted feelings about race to Rochester, Antoinette is also touching on another important issue: the question of national identity. That is, how do we determine who "belongs" in a country? Is it determined by race? Does whoever live there "first" get first dibs? Then neither black nor white can lay claim to the islands, because the Caribs and other indigenous tribes preceded them. Antoinette's musings here could indirectly explain why white Creoles attract so much abuse: their liminal status as not-quite-white and not-quite-black undercuts the claim that either race deserves to call the island exclusively theirs.

*I remember saying in a voice that was not like my own that it was too light. (II.3.3.88)*

Thought: At this point, Rochester has been drugged with obeah powder by Antoinette. He enters into a zombie-esque state where he temporarily loses his sense of self. However, the passage also invites us to think about the other ways in which Rochester becomes a zombie, so to speak. Is Rochester, who considers himself superior to everyone else because he's a white European male, really so different from people like Antoinette and Christophine?

*"Bertha is not my name. You are trying to make me into someone else, calling me by another name. I know, that's obeah too." (II.6.6.31)*

Thought: Antoinette learns Christophine's lesson about the way that the white-dominated, colonial society works. (See our discussion of Quote #8 under "Race.") Rochester's calling Antoinette another name isn't just an annoying habit. It's his way of taking control over her entire identity, just as he assumed legal control over her fortune when he married her. Rochester's "obeah" makes us wonder whether he's all that different from Christophine…

*"She is not béké like you, but she is béké, and not like us either." (II.6.7.52)*

Thought: Christophine tries to explain Antoinette's ambiguous racial status to Rochester, but even Christophine, who seems wordy enough when she's abusing Rochester, can't seem to find the right words to explain exactly what Antoinette *is*. At the same time that she tries to explain Antoinette's Creole temperament, she risks repelling Rochester because it's Antoinette's Creole side that really turns him off. Perhaps this is the game Christophine wants to play – who knows what she really wants?

*I scarcely recognized her voice. No warmth, no sweetness. The doll had a doll's voice, a breathless but curiously indifferent voice. (II.8.25)*

Thought: To Rochester, Antoinette has become a "doll," an inanimate object. But you could say that he's been objectifying her all along. At this point in the novel, the end of Part II, it's up for debate as to whether Rochester has completed his domination of Antoinette, or whether Antoinette's doll-like exterior is only a sham, a mask to conceal her rebellious impulses.

*There is no looking-glass here and I don't know what I am like now [...] The girl I saw was myself not quite myself. Long ago when I was a child and very lonely I tried to kiss her. But the glass was between us – hard, cold, and misted over with my breath. Now they have taken everything away. What am I doing in this place and who am I? (III.3.2)*

Thought: Locked up in Thornfield Hall, Antoinette has no access to a mirror, part of Rochester's strategy for depriving her of a unique identity to call her own. The childhood mirror scene she describes here is reminiscent of the scene with Tia (see our discussion of Quote #2 above): her sense of alienation from the image of herself indicates her general lack of a sense of self. But this quote also brings up the larger question of whether Antoinette is in fact "mad" – has she really lost her mind? Or can we see her fractured sense of self as a consequence of her personal history? Perhaps we have to learn to "read" Antoinette in a way that Rochester, or any of the other characters, never could.

*I heard the parrot call as he did when he saw a stranger, Qui est là? Qui est là? And the man who hated me was calling too, Bertha! Bertha! [...] But when I looked over the edge I saw the pool at Coulibri. Tia was there. She beckoned to me and when I hesitated, she laughed [...] Someone screamed and I thought, Why did I scream? I called "Tia!" and jumped and woke. (III.7.6)*

Thought: These lines are from the end of Antoinette's recurring dream. Here it sounds as if, in answer to the question "*Qui est là?*" ("Who is there?"), Antoinette's answer isn't Antoinette or Bertha, but Tia. A mark of her identification with Tia, her hostile childhood "friend"? If so, does that mean she's waking up *as* Tia? Are we supposed to read her burning down the house as being somehow motivated by her identification with Tia, a black female character? Or does her calling out "Tia!" reflect the persistent splitting of her self, closing off the possibility of ever having an identity to call her own? Hmm....

## Language and Communication Quotes

*It was their talk about Christophine that changed Coulibri, not the repairs or the new furniture or the strange faces. Their talk about Christophine and obeah changed it. (I.1.6.1)*

Thought: This quote refers to the power that gossip has, in part because it's the voice of a community, the "they." The second sentence in the quote is kind of odd because it could be read two ways: either the talk about Christophine and the talk about obeah changed Coulibri, or the talk about Christophine and obeah itself (not just the talk about obeah) changed Coulibri.

*[Christophine] had a quiet voice and a quiet laugh (when she did laugh), and though she could speak good English if she wanted to, and French as well as patois, she took care to talk as they talked. (I.1.2.9)*

Thought: Christophine shows here an awareness of how language marks a person's place in society. Even though she can speak "good" English, she knows that to assimilate with the black Jamaican community, she has to speak English in the same way they do.

*Say nothing and it may not be true. (II.2.5.20)*

Thought: This quote is more a statement of a wish than a fact, isn't it? Given the corrosive effects of gossip in Antoinette's life – think of everything that was said about her father, her mother, and her brother – her desire is understandable.

*So I was told, but I have noticed that negroes as a rule refuse to discuss the black magic in which so many believe. Voodoo as it is called in Haiti – Obeah in some of the islands, another name in South Africa. They confuse matters by telling lies if pressed. (II.4.3.28)*

Thought: The unnamed author here discusses the problems he has getting information about obeah, but the quote also shows how important speech *and* silence is to the way obeah works. Obeah's magic has a scientific explanation (the "untraceable" powder, a poison), but everyone, white and black, treats it as if it were actually effective magic. Otherwise, why would Christophine be imprisoned for practicing obeah? Talk about what it does is critical to obeah's power on the whole community's imagination, but silence about how it actually works, about the scientific explanation for how it works, contributes to its mystique.

*"Yes, that was his story, and is any of it true?" I said, cold and calm. [...]*

*"But we must talk about it." Her voice was high and shrill.*

*"Only if you promise to be reasonable."*

*But this is not the place or the time, I thought [...] "Not tonight," I said again. "Some other time."*

*"I might never be able to tell you in any other place or at any other time. No other time, now. You frightened?" she said, imitating a negro's voice, singing and insolent. (II.6.3.26, 29-32)*

Thought: The passage shows how, at a critical point in Antoinette and Rochester's relationship, true dialogue fails, and in a sense, language fails. Instead of being able to approach the conversation as two equals, they are both stymied by their own assumptions about each other. No matter what she says, Antoinette will always be a hysterical, irrational woman to Rochester, and, no matter what he says, Rochester will always be the cold, unfeeling man to Antoinette. Antoinette's taking on a "negro's voice" here is as much a taunt as her recognition that Rochester has placed her in the same exploitable racial category as Amélie. With all this baggage, how can there ever be a "right" time to talk?

*"Lies are never forgotten, they go on and they grow." (II.6.3.42)*

Thought: Antoinette relates here her experience that sometimes the past is forgotten to the point that only myths and fictions remain – perhaps myths and fictions survive because they serve the needs of the present. This point touches on the project of the novel as a whole to recover the story of Bertha Mason, the madwoman of *Jane Eyre*, to look behind Rochester's version of events and get the story from Bertha's perspective.

*"She tell me in the middle of all this you start calling her names. Marionette. Some word so."*

*"Yes, I remember, I did."*

*(Marionnete, Antoinette, Marionetta, Antoinetta)*

*"That word mean doll, eh? Because she won't speak. You want to force her to cry and to speak."*

*(Force her to cry and to speak)*

*"But she won't [...] You meant her to hear."*

*Yes, that didn't just happen. I meant it.*

*(I lay awake all night long after they were asleep, and as soon as it was light I got up and dressed and saddled Preston. And I came to you. Oh Christophine. O Pheena, Pheena, help me.) (II.6.7.37-44)*

Thought: This quote is from one of the strangest passages in the book (and that's saying a lot). The novel doesn't really help us out with explaining whether the italicized passages are bits of Rochester's interior monologue, bits of Christophine's dialogue echoing in Rochester's head, or something completely different, like the part in the parenthesis above, which sounds like Antoinette. Is Christophine performing some kind of obeah mind meld on Rochester, funneling Antoinette's appeal straight into his head? Or is Rochester just taking an imaginative leap? The structure of the passage invites us to consider how much of Rochester's actions – and reactions – are being "programmed" by Christophine.

*[Christophine] is intelligent in her way and can express herself well, but I did not like the look of her at all, and consider her a most dangerous person. My wife insisted that she had gone back to Martinique her native island, and was very upset that I had mentioned the matter even in such a roundabout fashion. (II.5.19)*

Thought: As Mr. Fraser's letter indicates, Christophine is considered dangerous really not for any rational reason – "the look of her"? How vague can he get? It's the *talk* about what she can do that contributes to her power in Jamaican society.

*"What you do with her money, eh?" Her voice was still quiet but with a hiss in it when she said "money." I thought, of course, that is what all the rigamarole is about. I no longer felt dazed, tired, half-hypnotized, but alert and wary, ready to defend myself. (II.6.7.75)*

Thought: The word "money" is the magic word that pops Rochester out of his odd trance-like dialogue with Christophine. Whether it's because money is all he cares about or because he's had an epiphany about Christophine's true aims is questionable.

*It is in your mind to pretend she is mad. I know it. The doctors say what you tell them to say. That man Richard he say what you want him to say – glad and willing too, I know. She will be like her mother. You do that for money? But you wicked like Satan self! (II.6.7.98)*

Thought: Christophine's interest in Antoinette may or may not be purely altruistic, but she seems to have a point here. By virtue of his position in society, Rochester has the medical community on his side, and they have the power to declare Antoinette insane simply by saying so. As a Creole, a woman, and now declared mentally ill, Antoinette is triply subordinated to Rochester's will.

*Very soon she'll join all the others who know the secret and will not tell it. Or cannot. Or try and fail because they do not know enough. They can be recognized. White faces, dazed eyes, aimless gestures, high-pitched laughter […] I too can wait – for the day when she is only a memory to be avoided, locked away, and like all memories a legend. Or a lie. (II.8.36)*

Thought: Rochester has learned Antoinette's lesson (in Quote #5 above) about lies a little *too* well. The "secret" of who she really is doesn't matter; it's her legend that matters. It's hard not to see here a wink at *Jane Eyre*, where Bertha is just such a "memory to be avoided, locked away." But before we buy into Rochester as the quintessential all-powerful European male too quickly, shouldn't we consider how Rochester seems to be borrowing the techniques of the people around him – Antoinette, Christophine? He seems to be affected by their way of looking at the world – you could say taking the very words out of their mouths, no? What's *that* all about?

## Love Quotes

*I learnt to say very quickly as the others did, "offer up all the prayers, works and sufferings of this day." But what about happiness, I thought at first, is there no happiness? There must be. Oh happiness, of course, happiness, well. But I soon forgot about happiness. (I.2.5.1)*

Thought: At the convent, Antoinette questions the overwhelming emphasis on happiness as possible only in the afterlife – i.e., after death, in heaven.

*The saints we hear about were all very beautiful and wealthy. All loved by rich and handsome young men. [...] and [Mother St. Justine] slides on to order and chastity, that flawless crystal that, once broken, can never be mended. (I.2.4.2-3)*

Thought: As part of her religious education, Antoinette hears a lot of stories about young maidens who choose a life "married" to their God as opposed to hot young men. These stories reinforce what she learned from her mother's unhappy marriage to Mr. Mason: romantic love isn't possible, and sexual desire can only corrupt and degrade.

*"I'll trust you if you'll trust me. Is that a bargain?" (II.2.26)*

Thought: We feel compelled to repeat here that *maybe* Rochester isn't such a terrible guy. (Doesn't really help the novel if he's just a one-sided, flat-out-mean villain, right?) In an honorable mood, Rochester touches on the one thing that Antoinette and he both need if their marriage is to survive: mutual trust. Of course, the rest of the novel is just a long series of betrayals, but at least he made an effort.

*"If I could die. Now, when I am happy. Would you do that? Would you do that? You wouldn't have to kill me. Say die and I will die. You don't believe me? Then try, try say die and watch me die."*

*"Die then! Die!" I watched her die many times. In my way, not in hers [...] Very soon she was as eager for what's called loving as I was – more lost and drowned afterwards. (II.3.5.40-1)*

Thought: Antoinette and Rochester's sex talk might seem weird and more than a little morbid, but they're playing on a literary tradition of using death as a metaphor for orgasm. (See "Shout Outs," Othello.) But Rochester here is careful to distinguish between love and sex, "what's called loving," and furthermore, between his way of "dying" and hers. It seems that his way of dying is sex, but Antoinette's words seems to indicate that she associates dying with happiness. In contrast to the convent, where happiness is associated with chastity, Antoinette is experimenting with happiness as sexual desire. But with death as the dominant metaphor, neither Rochester nor Antoinette seem to have a particularly appealing attitude toward sex.

*"When man don't love you, more you try, more he hate you, man like that. If you love them they treat you bad, if you don't love them they after you night and day bothering your soul case out." (II.5.1.14)*

Thought: Really, what's there to say? Christophine is just uttering one of those clichés that are still around because they have a tiny kernel of truth. You know, the "rules," playing hard-to-get, "he's just not into you," etc. But Christophine is also touching on here the basic problem with the way Rochester's desire works – he seeks to *own* things, to possess Antoinette. Once she's his, he loses interest because he doesn't need to pursue her anymore.

*That was the first thing I asked her – about the powder. I asked what it was. She said it was to keep the cockroaches away […] I had never seen her look so gay or so beautiful. She poured wine into two glasses and handed me one but I swear it was before I drank that I longed to bury my face in her hair as I used to do. I said, "We are letting ghosts trouble us. Why shouldn't we be happy?" (II.6.3.87-88)*

Thought: In one of his moments of tenderness, Rochester brings up an interesting question: how much does Antoinette contribute to the situation? Without a doubt, locking up a woman in your attic is a pretty extreme and degrading thing to do, but isn't drugging your husband kind of a no-no? Just as Christophine said, explaining things to Rochester seems to have softened him up – he even uses that word, "happy," that Antoinette's been obsessing over for the entire novel. But perhaps Antoinette was just so convinced of Rochester's malevolent intentions that she couldn't help but drug him? Then why did Christophine give Antoinette the obeah powder in the first place? This passage brings up all kinds of questions about Antoinette's *and* Christophine's motivations.

*"I hate [the place] now like I hate you and before I die I will show you how much I hate you." (II.6.6.33)*

Thought: It's interesting that Antoinette and Rochester never express their love to each other, and Antoinette is more ready to express her love for a place than for a person (see our discussion of Quote #1 in "Identity.") But we also have to wonder how different Antoinette's hatred is from her love for Rochester. She drugged him *before* he betrayed her with Amélie, just on the mere suspicion that he *might* leave her. Who needs love like that?

*She'll not dress up and smile at herself in that damnable looking-glass [...] I'll take her in my arms, my lunatic. She's mad but  mine, mine. What will I care for gods or devils or for Fate itself. If she smiles or weeps or both. For me. (II.7.13, 17)*

Thought: As with Antoinette, Rochester's love doesn't seem to be too different from his hate. For Rochester, both emotions seem to be essentially possessive, appropriative emotions: he wants to own her completely, and her fortune and her body are not enough. He has to own her entire sense of self, but to do that, he has to destroy her sanity.

*All the mad conflicting emotions had gone and left me wearied and empty. Sane. [...] I hated [the island's] beauty and its magic and the cruelty which was part of its loveliness. Above all I hated her. For she belonged to the magic and the loveliness. She had left me thirsty and all my life would be thirst and longing for what I had lost before I found it. (II.8.33-4)*

Thought: Here we get some insight into how love and hate can be so closely intertwined for Rochester. If he seeks to own Antoinette body and soul, it's to fill a void within himself, his "thirst and longing for what I had lost before I found it." Just as Tia indicated for Antoinette what she had lost (a concrete racial identity) before she had found it, Antoinette indicates for Rochester something critical to the way he thinks of himself, something that he didn't know he lacked until he met her. Now what that something might be is a huge question that he doesn't seem to answer or be able to answer, mired as he is in all those "mad conflicting emotions." But even though Rochester is repulsed by Antoinette, he still *needs* her as a reminder of what that something is. Confusing as this all is, it partly explains why he doesn't just throw her out and washes his hands of her altogether.

*That was the life and death kiss and you only know a long time afterwards what it is, the life and death kiss. (III.5.8)*

Thought: Antoinette describes her last kiss with Sandi Cosway. We never really get to know Sandi in the novel, but in the few instances we do see him, he seems to be a presence that offers Antoinette security, safety – well, happiness, really. So why didn't she run away with him?

## Mortality Quotes

*"I dare say we would have died if [Christophine]'d turned against us and that would have been a better fate. To die and be forgotten and at peace. Not to know that one is abandoned, lied about, helpless." (I.1.2.12)*

Thought: Antoinette inherits her mother's morbid way of looking at the world, expressed in the quote above. To die isn't about merely ceasing to exist, but more importantly, to lose the *awareness* that you may as well be dead. The quote also brings up the interesting question as to why Christophine is so invested in keeping Annette and her family alive when they have no fortune to speak of at the time. Christophine may be performing a kind of obeah in the sense

that she is supporting Annette and her family when they are socially dead, turning them into social zombies, if you will.

*When I asked Christophine what happened when you died, she said, "You want to know too much." (I.1.7.33)*

Thought: Antoinette reveals here an early obsession with death that will continue into her adult life, most notably in her relationship with Rochester.

*I could hardly wait for all this ecstasy and once I prayed for a long time to be dead. (I.2.5.3)*

Thought: Antoinette's experience with religion is problematic because it seems to prey on her most morbid tendencies. If heaven is such a good time, then why stick around on earth?

*Always this talk of death. (Is she trying to tell me that is the secret of this place? That there is no other way? She knows. She knows.)*

*"Why did you make me want to live? Why did you do that to me?"*

*"Because I wished it. Isn't that enough?"*

*"Yes, it is enough. But if one day you didn't wish it. What should I do then? Suppose you took this happiness away when I wasn't looking…" (II.3.5.32-5)*

Thought: Here we have another instance of a character keeping another character alive, only this time it's Rochester who's working the "obeah." Antoinette ascribes to Rochester an almost magical power over her state of mind and her life. For Rochester, on the other hand, death is associated with the "secret of this place." The location is felt as a threat to his selfhood, just as Antoinette is.

*I wonder if she ever guessed how near she came to dying. In her way, not in mine. It was not a safe game to play – in that place. Desire, Hatred, Life, Death came very close in the darkness. (II.3.5.55)*

Thought: This quote gives us a different inflection on what it means to die in "her way" than we get in Quote #4, in our discussion of "Love." While previously Antoinette linked death with happiness, here Rochester reads "her way" of dying as something far riskier, as an actual physical death. Is sex really a kind of death where the two lose control over themselves in sexual union? In such a state, isn't it possible for one person to exploit the other's temporary loss of control and take over? What would it mean to use a different metaphor for sex – say, life? In a sense, the "game," and the sex act itself, is a life-and-death battle over what terms such as love and happiness mean.

*There are always two deaths, the real one and the one people know about. (II.6.3.19)*

Thought: Antoinette explains to Rochester how she felt her mother died a symbolic death when the Coulibri estate burned down and her brother died, well before her mother's actual physical death. There are many ways of dying or ceasing to exist, some that are private, secret, or otherwise inexpressible, as the tragic events in the novel bear out.

*I woke in the dark after dreaming that I was buried alive, and when I was awake the feeling of suffocation persisted. (II.6.4.1)*

Thought: After being poisoned, Rochester experiences a kind of zombie state by experiencing death while he's still alive. It begs the question as to whether his behavior following this scene (for example, his sleeping with Amélie) is the result of the drug, and, if so, whether he's really responsible for his actions.

*She was only a ghost. A ghost in the grey daylight. Nothing left but hopelessness. Say die and I will die. Say die and watch me die. (II.8.23)*

Thought: Antoinette's words return to Rochester as he contemplates her at the end of Part II. The term "ghost" is a nod to _Jane Eyre_, where Bertha Mason is mistaken for a ghost. Antoinette's ghostliness in this scene bears witness to her own symbolic death, thus paralleling her mother's fate.

*It was then that I saw her – the ghost. The woman with streaming hair. She was surrounded by a gilt frame but I knew her. (III.7.3)*

Thought: Like Quote #8, this quote is also a reference to Bertha Mason's ghostliness in _Jane Eyre_. Interestingly, Antoinette doesn't recognize the ghost in the mirror as her own reflection. It seems at this point that Rochester's plan to obliterate her sense of self – a symbolic death – has succeeded.

*Someone screamed and I thought, Why did I scream? I called "Tia!" and jumped and woke. (III.7.6)*

Thought: For a fuller discussion of the ending, see "What's Up with the Ending?" But in the context of our discussion of the theme of mortality here, this passage is interesting for suggesting an up side to death. We know, we know, there's an _up_ side? Well, look, death can be understood as a loss of selfhood, right? What if that selfhood was a mess of half-conscious racist assumptions? _Maybe_ Antoinette's loss of self is the loss of a racist self, an enabling loss in the sense that it makes possible her full acceptance of Tia. It's a big maybe, but a maybe worth trying out…

## The Supernatural Quotes

*I was suddenly very much afraid [...] I was certain that hidden in the room (behind the old black press?) there was a dead man's dried hand, white chicken feathers, a cock with its throat cut, dying slowly, slowly. Drop by drop the blood was falling into a red basin and I imagined I could hear it. No one had every spoken to me about obeah – but I knew what I would find if I dared to look. Then Christophine came in smiling and pleased to see me. Nothing alarming ever happened and I forgot, or told myself I had forgotten. (I.1.6.3)*

Thought: This quote is awfully strange because Antoinette seems to know without knowing that there's an obeah charm in the room. How does she know what a charm looks like if nobody's ever talked about it? Is it possible that she's repressed what she's heard, just as she tells herself in the passage above that she's forgotten what she's seen in Christophine's room? The passage above is a great one to look at if you want to try to disentangle the weird dynamic of rumor and denial that goes into obeah's mystique.

*I heard someone say something about bad luck and remembered that it was very unlucky to kill a parrot, or even to see a parrot die. (I.1.8.19)*

Thought: It seems ridiculous that a parrot on fire could dispel a riot, but there you have it. The scene attests to the way superstitions operate: what a community *believes* to be true can generate its own objective reality.

*But we have our own Saint, the skeleton of a girl of fourteen under the altar of the convent chapel. The Relics. But how did the nuns get them out there, I ask myself? In a cabin trunk? Specially packed for the hold? How? But here she is, and St. Innocenzia is her name. We do not know her story; she is not in the book. (I.2.4.2)*

Thought: The novel creates its own mythical saint to suggest an analogy with Antoinette, who herself gets locked up in the hold of a ship and gets transported in the opposite direction – to England and Europe, rather than the Caribbean. The convent's worship of a girl's skeleton invites parallels with obeah rituals (the dried, shriveled hand of Quote #1 above). These similarities suggest that the lines separating obeah from Christianity, black magic from religion, are not quite so clear-cut as they appear.

*So many things are sins, why? Another sin, to think that. However, happily, Sister Marie Augustine says thoughts are not sins, if they are driven away at once. You say Lord save me, I perish. I find it very comforting to know exactly what must be done. All the same, I did not pray so often after that and soon, hardly at all. I felt bolder, happier, more free. But not so safe. (I.2.5.3)*

Thought: Again, Antoinette's religious education contains magical elements. "Lord save me, I perish" is Antoinette's *abracadabra*, the magical password that drives away her sins, but it also echoes Christophine's ominous mumbling in Quote #9.

*Turning around she saw me and laughed loudly. "Your husban' he outside the door and he looked like he see zombi. Must be he tired of the sweet honeymoon too." (II.4.1.32)*

Thought: By claiming that Rochester looks as if he's seen a zombie (i.e., Antoinette), Amélie suggests that zombies are not mythical creatures, but can refer to anyone who has undergone some traumatic event. In this way, Amélie demystifies the mystique –and the terror – a zombie generates by reducing the term to a casual insult.

*I had reached the forest and you cannot mistake the forest. It is hostile […] Under the orange trees I noticed little bunches of flowers tied with grass. (II.4.3.2)*

Thought: Lost in the forest, Rochester comes across an obeah offering, emphasizing obeah's close association with the land itself.

*A zombi is a dead person who seems to be alive or a living person who is dead. A zombi can also be the spirit of a place, usually malignant but sometimes to be propitiated with sacrifices or offerings of flowers and fruit […] They cry out in the wind that is their voice, they rage in the sea that is their anger. (II.4.3.28)*

Thought: On reading about obeah, Rochester realizes that the flowers he saw in Quote #6 was one such offering to appease the ghost of Père Lilievre, who was rumored to haunt the area. But the passage also asks us to consider what characters also serve as spirits who have to be plied with flowers and fruit, that "cry out" and "rage" – yup, that's Antoinette we're talking about. Makes you take a second look at all those flowers in their honeymoon house, doesn't it?

*"So you believe in that tim-tim story about obeah, you hear when you so high? All that foolishness and folly. Too besides, that is not for béké. Bad, bad trouble come when béké meddle with that." (II.5.1.37)*

Thought: Christophine's words are somewhat disingenuous here because she does end up giving Antoinette an obeah potion. But her words are also loaded in that she's already been imprisoned by the *békés*, or whites, for practicing obeah, which was associated with slave mutinies, particularly in Haiti. Obeah terrifies precisely because it's a cultural expression, not a magical one: the voice of protest for a community, not a species of witchcraft or wizardry. Christophine's use of the word "trouble" also echoes the first line of the novel, where "trouble" refers to the turmoil after the Emancipation Act was passed in 1833.

*She said something I did not hear. Then she took a sharp stick and drew lines and circles on the earth under the tree, then rubbed them out with her foot.*

*"If you talk to him first I do what you ask me." (II.5.2.9)*

Thought: This quote shows how Christophine's obeah works as much through psychological manipulation as it does through its various incantations, rituals, and potions. Christophine gives Antoinette a condition that Christophine has no way of enforcing: once she's given up the potion, there's no way to stop Antoinette from doing whatever she wants with it, whether she talks to Rochester or not. Christophine's words throughout their exchange seems to indicate that she knows what will happen – "bad, bad trouble" – if Antoinette uses the powder. Then why does she give Antoinette the powder? Her intentions continue to remain mysterious.

*I drank some more rum and, drinking, I drew a house surrounded by trees. A large house. I divided the third floor into rooms and in one room I drew a standing woman – a child's scribble, a dot for a head, a larger one for the body, a triangle for a skirt, slanting lines for arms and feet. But it was an English house. (II.6.8.17)*

Thought: There's an awful lot of drinking in the novel, and you could say that rum and alcohol like the obeah powder alter states of mind. Christophine's obeah seems to have seeped into Rochester's consciousness here as he too draws shapes (see Quote #9) in order to influence reality. His clumsy sketch here provides a blueprint for his eventual confinement of Antoinette to his manor house.

## Power Quotes

*"Of course they have their own misfortunes. Still waiting for this compensation the English promised when the Emancipation Act was passed. Some will wait for a long time." (I.1.1.3)*

Thought: The novel sets the historical mood of the novel by mentioning the Emancipation Act on the very first page. By associating emancipation with "misfortunes," the novel explores how true freedom is impossible given the persistent social, political, and economic inequities on the island. (See "Setting" for a fuller discussion of the historical significance of the Act.)

*No more slavery! She had to laugh! "These new ones have Letter of the Law. Same thing. They got magistrate. They got fine. They got jail house and chain gang. They got tread machine to mash up people's feet. New ones worse than old ones – more cunning, that's all." (I.1.3.25)*

Thought: Christophine's cynicism reflects her own experience with the continuing racial injustice on the island. While blacks are no longer enslaved, they are persecuted in other ways by being treated as inferior citizens under the law. The use of the law is in some ways more hypocritical than slavery, because the law professes to be the expression of an idea of justice, while the institution of slavery didn't have such lofty moral pretensions.

*My stepfather talked about a plan to import labourers – coolies he called them – from the East Indies. When Myra had gone out, Aunt Cora said, "I shouldn't discuss that if I were you. Myra is listening." (I.1.7.19)*

Thought: Mr. Mason's comments here suggest that the ensuing riot could be seen as a form of class-based anger on the part of the black community. By importing laborers, Mr. Mason would be withholding jobs from the black community, further aggravating conditions of economic hardship.

*"It's disgraceful," [Aunt Cora] said. "It's shameful. You are handing over everything the child owns to a perfect stranger. Your father would never have allowed it. She should be protected, legally. A settlement can be arranged and it should be arranged." (II.5.2.1)*

Thought: Just as Christophine criticizes the law for its unfair treatment of blacks, Aunt Cora criticizes the law for its treatment of women as minors, as the subjects of their husbands, and demands legal protection for Antoinette.

*"Then I will have the police up, I warn you. There must be some law and order even in this God-forsaken island."*

*"No police here," she said. "No chain gang, no tread machine, no dark jail either. This is free country and I am free woman."*

*"Christophine," I said, "you lived in Jamaica for years, and you know Mr. Fraser, the Spanish Town magistrate, well. I wrote to him about you. Would you like to hear what he answered?" (II.6.6.93)*

Thought: By appealing to the police, Rochester aligns himself with the law (i.e. the political authority on the islands), the same authority that Christophine criticizes – almost word for word – in Quote #2. Rochester's reference to the law has an almost magical effect on Christophine as she immediately shuts up. Christophine's words also indicate why she remains in the British-occupied islands of the Caribbean, rather than in Martinique, the French colony she's originally from. At the time, slavery is still legal in the French empire, and she wouldn't be a "free woman."

*"I thought you liked the black people so much," [Antoinette] said, still in that mincing voice, "but that's just a lie like everything else. You like the light brown girls better, don't you? You abused the planters and made up stories about them, but you do the same thing. You send the girl away quicker, and with no money or less money, and that's all the difference."*

*"Slavery was not a matter of liking or disliking," I said, trying to speak calmly. "It was a question of justice."*

*"Justice," she said. "I've heard that word. It's a cold word. I tried it out," she said, still speaking in a low voice. "I wrote it down several times and always it looked like a damn cold lie to me. There is no justice." She drank some more rum and went on. "My mother whom you all talk about, what justice did she have? My mother sitting in the rocking-chair speaking about dead horses and dead grooms and a black devil kissing her sad mouth. Like you kissed mine."*

*(II.6.6.26)*

Thought: In this quote, Antoinette chastises Rochester for his hypocrisy in sleeping with Amélie. Rochester tries to take the high road by talking about slavery as an abstract human rights issue, but Antoinette here voices the uncomfortable truth that the abolition of slavery didn't lead to the abolition of racial inequality on the island. She also compares Rochester and the man who was hired to take care of her mother. You might remember that Antoinette witnessed her mother's caretaker raping her mother (II.6.3). Antoinette is suggesting here that although Rochester is supposed to be the responsible husband who takes care of his wife, he is in fact figuratively raping her by taking her fortune and having sex with her without loving her. Imitating Rochester's English accent – the "mincing voice" – is part of her rhetorical strategy to rub his face in his own duplicity.

*After all the house is big and safe, a shelter from the world outside which, say what you like, can be a black and cruel world to a woman. (III.1.2)*

Thought: This passage from Grace Poole's narrative suggests her feeling of solidarity with Antoinette's fate, a feeling of solidarity that reaches across racial and cultural lines. This passage puts another twist on Brontë's *Jane Eyre* by implying that Grace Poole both consciously and unconsciously helped Antoinette wreak her revenge on both Richard Mason and Rochester.

*"It was when he said 'legally' that you flew at him and when he twisted the knife out of your hand you bit him." (III.4.25)*

Thought: As we saw in Quote #7, nothing ticks off Antoinette quite so much as when men bring up justice and the law to justify their exploitation of women, whether it's Rochester sleeping with Amélie or Richard signing Antoinette's fortune over to Rochester.

*But I looked at the dress on the floor and it was as if the fire had spread across the room. It was beautiful and it reminded me of something I must do. I will remember I thought. I will remember quite soon now. (III.6.10)*

Thought: The red dress serves as a concrete reminder for Antoinette of her task, which is never explicitly stated, but could be a reference to her vow to show Rochester exactly how much she hates him in Part II (II.6.6.33). The red dress's association with Antoinette's femininity and fire, which recalls the fire at Coulibri, suggests that the red dress is kind of a call to arms for Antoinette, an appeal for her to use the same mode of protest that the blacks used against Mr. Mason earlier in the novel. (See our discussion of Quote #3 above.) This connection is further stressed in the next section when Antoinette dreams of setting fire to Thornfield Hall.

## Versions of Reality Quotes

*I went to bed early and slept at once. I dreamed that I was walking in the forest. Not alone. Someone who hated me was with me, out of sight. I could hear heavy footsteps coming closer and though I struggled and screamed I could not move. (I.1.3.27)*

Thought: This passage describes the first instance of Antoinette's recurring nightmare, which is brought on by the events of the day: her fight with Tia and her encounter with her mother's guests, the Luttrells, who will eventually introduce her to her future husband, Mr. Mason. The generally hostile environment of the dream, the threat from an unnamed and unseen stranger, and Antoinette's paralysis all foreshadow Antoinette's eventual confinement in Rochester's English manor.

*Again I have left the house at Coulibri. It is still night and I am walking towards the forest. I am wearing a long dress and thin slippers, so I walk with difficulty, following the man who is with me and holding up the skirt of my dress. It is white and beautiful and I don't wish to get it soiled. I follow him, sick with fear, but I make no effort to save myself; if anyone were to try to save me, I would refuse. This must happen. Now we have reached the forest. We are under the tall dark trees and there is no wind. "Here?" He turns and looks at me, his face black with hatred, and when I see this I begin to cry. (I.2.5.24)*

Thought: Just as Antoinette's first dream precedes Annette's marriage to Mr. Mason, Antoinette's second dream precedes her own impending marriage, this time orchestrated by Mr. Mason. The second dream further elaborates on the first dream. The white dress is a color associated with her mother, who loved wearing white, but the fact that it trails on the floor looks forward to Christophine, who also walks with her dress trailing on the floor, much to Rochester's disapproval (II.3.3.5). As the dream progresses, Antoinette ends up in a garden surrounded by a stone wall and hugs a tree that tries to shake her off. This scene looks ahead to Rochester's comparison of his hatred to a hurricane bending a tree (II.7.12).

*Reality might disconcert her, bewilder her, hurt her, but it would not be reality. It would be only a mistake, a misfortune, a wrong path taken, her fixed ideas would never change. (II.3.5.53)*

Thought: Here, Rochester expresses a rather condescending opinion of Antoinette. He differentiates himself from what he calls her lack of realism, without acknowledging that he too has certain fixed ideas – about women and race, for example – that don't change even if proven otherwise.

*I had reached the forest and you cannot mistake the forest. It is hostile. The path was overgrown but it was possible to follow it […] The track led to a large clear space. Here were the ruins of a stone house and round the ruins rose trees that had grown to an incredible height […] I was lost and afraid among these enemy trees, so certain of danger that when I heard footsteps and a shout I did not answer. The footsteps and the voice came nearer. (II.4.3.2-3)*

**Wide Sargasso Sea**
**Shmoop Learning Guide**

Thought: What's odd about reading this passage out of context is that it sounds like one of Antoinette's dreams, but it's not – it's *Rochester*, the same guy who dismissed her version of reality in Quote #3 above. And the passage doesn't describe a dream, but his actual experience getting lost in the forests around Granbois.

*I must know more than I know already. For I know that house where I will be cold and not belonging, the bed I shall lie in has red curtains, and I have slept there many times before, long ago. How long ago? In that bed I will dream the end of my dream. But my dream had nothing to do with England and I must not think like this, I must remember about chandeliers and dancing, about swans and roses and snow. (II.5.1.26)*

Thought: Antoinette's musings here foreshadow her eventual confinement in England in Part III of the novel. But it also brings up some interesting questions about her control over her own fate. How can she "foretell" the future? Why *must* these things happen to her, or does she have the power to change her destiny?

*There would be the sky and the mountains, the flowers and the girl and the feeling that all this was a nightmare, the faint consoling hope that I might wake up. (II.6.1.9)*

Thought: Again, Rochester doesn't seem to acknowledge how similar he is to Antoinette with his fixed ideas. Rochester, like Antoinette, seems to be able to predict what's going to happen, as he "predicts" that Amélie is going to appear before him. Of course, he also called her to him, so no real mystery there. For Rochester, predictions confirm his sense of mastery over a situation, in contrast to Antoinette, who is terrified by what she foresees. He knows Amélie is going to appear because he has control over her. He's not surprised when he receives Daniel's letter because it confirms what he already suspects. If everything feels like a "nightmare," it's partly because the nightmare is his own creation.

*"Then she cursed me comprehensively, my eyes, my mouth, every member of my body, and it was like a dream in the large unfurnished room with the candles flickering and this red-eyed wild-haired stranger who was my wife shouting obscenities at me." (II.6.6.41)*

Thought: Rochester again feels as if he's in a dream, in an extraordinary situation that doesn't seem real. The subtext here is that Rhys is taking some of the words verbatim from *Jane Eyre*: is *Jane Eyre* then the "dream" in which all the characters are trapped?

*So I shall never understand why, suddenly, bewilderingly, I was certain that everything I had imagined to be truth was false. False. Only the magic and the dream are true – all the rest's a lie. Let it go. Here is the secret. Here. (II.8.6)*

Thought: Rochester has a brief epiphany about his life on the island. The fixed ideas – about his situation, Antoinette, the Caribbean – that were so entrenched in Quotes #3 and #6 seem to evaporate: he recognizes that what he believed to be "true" is actually only "imagined." Instead of approaching things as a rational, calculating, man, he has to learn to work with the "magic and the dream," whatever that means. We never find out, as the epiphany is short-lived and he's back to hating Antoinette.

*Only I know how long I have been here. Nights and days and days and nights, hundreds of them slipping through my fingers. But that does not matter. Time has no meaning. But something you can touch and hold like my red dress, that has a meaning. (III.4.30)*

Thought: Trapped in the attic, isolated from the world, Antoinette eschews conventional ways of thinking about space and time. Time isn't an abstract concept, but something you can finger, like a dress. Antoinette's musings here suggest that there are other, equally valid ways of understanding reality that might seem alien or just plain crazy to someone like Rochester.

*That was the third time I had my dream and it ended […] Then I turned around and saw the sky. It was red and all my life was in it […] Now at last I know why I was brought here and what I have to do. (III.7.1-6)*

Thought: For a more complete discussion of the ending, see our "What's Up with the Ending?" In the context of our discussion of "Versions of Reality" here, the last dream is interesting because it provides a condensed version of the events in the novel – kind of like a SportsCenter highlight reel. This scene suggests that there's more than one way of looking at reality, that sometimes reality is like a dream in that it can often be puzzling or illogical, a mix of familiar and unfamiliar elements. Of course the novel doesn't show us exactly what Antoinette ends up doing – that would be interpreting the dream for you, telling you what to think, and the novel is very much about letting you actively engage with the text and come up with your own interpretation.

## Contrasting Regions Quotes

*Our garden was large and beautiful as that garden in the Bible – the tree of life grew there. But it had gone wild. The paths were overgrown and a smell of dead flowers mixed with the fresh living smell. Underneath the tree ferns, tall as forest trees, the light was green. Orchids flourished out of reach or for some reason not to be touched. One was snaky looking, another like an octopus with long thin brown tentacles bare of leaves hanging from a twisted root. (I.1.2.2)*

Thought: This passage about the Coulibri estate makes explicit reference to the Biblical garden of Eden, but it's a strange and creepy paradise where beauty and decay are intermingled. Instead of being associated with a state of innocence, we have a "wild" paradise, with vaguely threatening flowers that look like snakes and octopi.

*There was a soft warm wind blowing but I understood why the porter had called it a wild place. Not only wild but menacing. Those hills could close in on you […] Everything is too much, I felt as I rode wearily after her. Too much blue, too much purple, too much green. The flowers too red, the mountains too high, the hills too near. (II.1.2.1-4)*

Thought: Rochester goes into sensory overload as he makes his way to Granbois. Unable to handle the "wild" beauty of the Caribbean, he finds it "menacing" as it threatens his control over his senses.

*"Oh England, England," she called back mockingly, and the sound went on and on like a warning I did not choose to hear.*

*Soon the road was cobblestoned and we stopped at a flight of stone steps. There was a large screw pine to the left and to the right what looked like an imitation of an English summer house. (II.1.2.12-13)*

Thought: For Rochester, the Caribbean takes him out of his English comfort zone, and thus radically challenges his sense of self. You can see how he clings to anything in the environment that remotely reminds him of England, as when he compares their vacation home to an "English summer house." Rather than appreciating the Caribbean on its own terms, he only sees the island as either a pale imitation or a monstrous deformation of his English homeland.

*"Is it true," she said, "that England is like a dream? Because one of my friends who married an Englishman wrote and told me so. She said this place London is like a cold dark dream sometimes. I want to wake up."*

*"Well," I answered annoyed, "that is precisely how your beautiful island seems to me, quite unreal and like a dream."*

Thought: Both characters spar over which country is more dream-like and "unreal" than the other, but Rochester gets annoyed, while Antoinette seems merely curious at this point. That Antoinette views England as merely a dream, and not the center of the universe, may have something to do with Rochester's annoyance.

*It was a beautiful place – wild, untouched, above all untouched, with an alien, disturbing, secret loveliness. And it kept its secret. I'd find myself thinking, "What I see is nothing – I want what it hides – that is not nothing." (II.3.4.4)*

Thought: In response to the "menacing" threat of his surroundings (see Quote #2 above), Rochester wants to figure out what makes it "alien, disturbing, secret," but *knowing* this secret seems equivalent to destroying what makes it so marvelous to begin with. That is, once it becomes familiar to him, it is no longer different and terrifying. Rochester also describes the location's disturbing beauty in the same way he describes Antoinette's appearance, particularly her eyes.

*She often questioned me about England and listened attentively to my answers, but I was certain that nothing I said made much difference. Her mind was already made up. Some romantic novel, a stray remark never forgotten, a sketch, a picture, a song, a waltz, some note of music, and her ideas were fixed. About England and about Europe. (II.3.5.53)*

Thought: Here the novel calls attention to Antoinette's ironic reversal of the way that the Caribbean is conceived in Victorian literature and English literature in general. Instead of the Caribbean being an exotic place made up of fictions and legends that have little to do with the "real" Caribbean, Antoinette sees England as just such a fantastic place.

*I will be a different person when I live in England and different things will happen to me […] England, rosy pink in the geography book map, but on the page opposite the words are closely crowded, heavy-looking. Exports, coal, iron, wool. Then imports and Character of Inhabitants. Names, Essex, Chelmsford on the Chelmer. The Yorkshire and Lincolnshire wolds. Wolds? Does that mean hills? How high? Half the height of ours, or not even that? (II.5.1.26)*

Thought: We see how Antoinette develops her image of England in this quote from Antoinette's point of view, rather than from Rochester's. And is it really any different than the way we learn about other countries – or even other states, for that matter – in school? In focusing on maps and unfamiliar names, Antoinette shows how much texts contribute to the way we get to know the world around us and, in a sense, limit our experience of the world as well.

*"England," said Christophine, who was watching me. "You think there is such a place?"*

*"How can you ask that? You know there is."*

*"I never see the damn place, how I know?"*

*"You do not believe that there is a country called England."*

*She blinked and answered quickly, "I don't say I don't   believe. I say I don't  know, I know what I see with my eyes and I never see it." (II.5.1.27-31)*

Thought: Christophine brings up an interesting distinction between believing and knowing, between a superficial and an intimate, lived knowledge of a region.

*Then I open the door and walk into their world. It is, as I always knew, made of cardboard. I have seen it before somewhere, this cardboard world where everything is coloured brown or dark red or yellow that has no light in it. As I walk along the passages I wish I could see what is behind the cardboard. They tell me I am in England but I don't believe them. We lost our way to England. When? Where? I don't remember, but we lost it. (III.3.5)*

Thought: Even though Antoinette is now actually in England, she still thinks of it as an imaginary place. In a sense, she's experiencing the distinction between belief and knowledge that Christophine lays out in Quote #9 above: since all she's seen of England is the interior of the house and a brief visit to a random meadow, how can she *know* she's in England? That the house is made out of paper reinforces the fact that, for Antoinette, England is still something straight out of the pages of a book. Like *Jane Eyre*, perhaps?

*That afternoon we went to England. There was grass and olive-green water and tall trees looking into the water. This, I thought, is England. If I could be here I'd get well again and the sound in my head would stop. (III.4.25)*

Thought: What's interesting about this passage is that England isn't a thoroughly horrible place, but actually has some redeeming features. The nature Antoinette describes invokes a typical English pastoral scene, a literary mode that celebrates England's natural beauty as representative of everything that's great about being English. For a novel that's a pretty obvious critique of British imperialism, it's interesting to think of what it finds redeeming about English culture. After all, it does adapt one of the greatest novels in the English literary tradition.

## Plot Analysis

## Classic Plot Analysis

### Initial Situation
*After Coulibri burns down, her brother dies, and her mother goes mad, Antoinette ends up in a convent school in Spanish Town, Jamaica.*
Part I of the novel does most of the work of setting up the initial situation for us. We learn about the host of factors that contribute to Antoinette's unstable childhood. With her father dead and her family's finances in shambles, Antoinette and her family occupy a kind of no-man's-land in Jamaican society. Shunned by both whites and blacks, they make do for a couple of years until Annette realizes one day that she doesn't have the resources to raise her children well. So she has to provide for them in the only way she can as a white Creole woman – get hitched to someone rich and white. Enter Mr. Mason. But instead of giving her family security, her marriage with Mr. Mason ends up costing Annette her home, her son, her sanity – and her life. Annette's tragic experience is, for Antoinette, a legacy of insecurity and deep skepticism – really, fear – of society and of love, of her sexuality and her sense of self.

### Conflict
*After a month of courtship, Antoinette marries Rochester.*
We know it's odd to describe a marriage as a conflict, but in Antoinette's turbulent world, marriage is an incredibly fraught thing. Marriage isn't a union of two people in love, but a financial arrangement manufactured by her stepfather and her stepbrother. Instead of insuring her security, her apparently well-intentioned stepfather's goal, Antoinette's wealth is signed

over to Rochester, thus resulting in her loss of economic freedom. To be fair, Rochester in the beginning seems to have some genuine feeling for Antoinette – remember the part where he promises to trust her if she trusts him? But whether this promise can withstand all the baggage they bring into the relationship...well, that's why their marriage is a conflict.

## Complication
*Rochester receives a nasty letter from Daniel Cosway/Boyd, Antoinette's alleged stepbrother, who claims all kinds of awful things about Antoinette and her family.*
Even though Daniel's letter is filled with all kinds of spiteful, self-aggrandizing comments that inspire skepticism in the reader, it preys on all of Rochester's insecurities. The fact that Antoinette's family *might* have a history of madness and degeneration brings out his ugly racial prejudices about Antoinette's being a white Creole. The fact that Antoinette *might* have had a relationship with Sandi Cosway brings out his own shame about having to marry someone for money and not for love, a luxury only the eldest son in the family can afford. Rochester isn't enraged after he receives the letter; he feels like it's saying something he already knows *precisely* because it plays on his insecurities. He doesn't really give Antoinette a chance to defend herself. From this point on, their course of their relationship has irrevocably changed.

## Climax
*Antoinette slips Rochester some voodoo Viagra, but it works a little too well – after sleeping with Antoinette, Rochester beds her maid.*
Yes, we realize that there is a sexual climax at the climax of this novel. In the novel, sex isn't just a physical act, but a battleground on which all of the forces that shape the characters collide; orgasm isn't just a physical consummation, but an assertion of power of one will over another. When Rochester ingests the obeah powder, he sleeps with Antoinette, but he's also rendered into a virtual zombie: he loses his will, his reason, his identity, the very feeling of being a live, sentient human being. He punishes Antoinette by sleeping with Amélie, who has openly mocked Antoinette for being a "white cockroach." Rochester's infidelity absolutely destroys Antoinette and her hopes for happiness.

## Suspense
*Distraught, Antoinette runs away to Christophine's, and, when she returns, she has an ugly quarrel with Rochester.*
The climax, or climaxes, of the novel generate(s) a series of reactions that worsen the situation. Instead of talking things over reasonably, everyone – Antoinette, Rochester, and to a lesser degree Christophine – seems to feed off each other's volatile emotions until they become lost in a blazing mess of acrimony. In such a state, neither Antoinette nor Rochester seems able to distinguish love from hate, and they both alternate between fiery rage and icy calm. It's difficult to know who to believe or who to sympathize with at this point.

## Denouement
*Rochester decides to ship Antoinette back to his manor in England.*
Rochester has Antoinette declared insane, ships her back to England, and locks her up in his attic. Confining her in this way is really only finishing off geographically what he's done to her on a physical and emotional level. Having already appropriated her fortune, he now lays claim to her entire person, symbolically indicated by the fact that he re-names her "Bertha." In Part III, Antoinette's narrative reflects this loss of self through her constant questioning of who and

where she is.

## Conclusion

*Antoinette has a dream where she sets fire to the entire house. When she wakes up, she escapes from her attic room and walks down a dark hallway by candlelight.*

While it may seem that the novel concludes with Antoinette's setting fire to Thornfield Hall, technically it's only in her dream where she sets fire to the house. The novel actually ends with Antoinette waking up from her dream and walking down a "dark passage." It's true that she says that she finally knows what she has to do, but she never specifies what this mysterious task is. For a fuller discussion of the ending, see our "What's Up with the Ending?" But let's just note here that the open-endedness of the ending seems fitting for a novel that has been driven by conflicting perspectives, a novel that has never given us readers the "truth" of what happened from an impartial or omniscient point of view. No one in the novel is exempt from its relentless perspectival clashing, not even the seemingly cool and calculating Rochester, and the novel isn't about to let us off the hook either.

## Booker's Seven Basic Plots Analysis: Tragedy

### Anticipation Stage

*After a difficult childhood, Antoinette comes of age in a convent school, where all the sermons about the blessed life after death make her wonder whether happiness is possible in this life.*

Due to the tragic circumstances of her early life, Antoinette enters into adulthood with serious questions about the possibility of happiness, particularly when it comes to romantic love. She's already seen how her mother's trust in Mr. Mason as a source of financial security and physical well-being was totally betrayed. In the convent, she's surrounded by a community of women who have effectively repressed any physical desire they have for the sake of a purely celibate, spiritual love. Mr. Mason's suggestion that Antoinette is now ready to be married understandably fills her with dread.

### Dream Stage

*Antoinette seems to have found happiness through a sexually satisfying relationship with her new husband, Rochester.*

In the early days of their marriage, Antoinette's fears about marriage seem unfounded. Rochester doesn't seem to be such a bad guy, and she starts to feel safe around him – so safe, in fact, that she enjoys a sexually satisfying relationship with him.

### Frustration Stage

*Antoinette's marriage soon sours when Rochester receives a letter filled with malicious gossip from Daniel Cosway/Boyd.*

Alas, there's no happy ending in sight for Antoinette. Her blissful honeymoon is interrupted when Rochester receives a letter from Daniel Cosway/Boyd, who makes all kinds of allegations about her family and her own previous romantic attachments.

### Nightmare Stage

*Convinced that sex is the only way to get Rochester to love her, Antoinette slips Rochester a*

*voodoo aphrodisiac, but he gets violently ill, and sleeps with her maid.*
Desperate to recover the happiness she had with Rochester in the early days of their marriage, Antoinette decides to drug him into having sex with her. Unfortunately, this plan backfires as he gets her back right where it hurts the most: sex with Amélie, a woman who has repeatedly insulted her. And even more painfully, she has to listen to the whole thing go down because she's in the next room.

### Destruction or Death Wish Stage
*To retaliate, Antoinette flirts with a number of men and has an affair with Sandi Cosway. Rochester has her declared insane and confines her to an attic room in his English manor, where she ultimately escapes with dreams of burning down the house and everyone in it.*
We've already discussed the problems with determining exactly what happens in the ending (See "What's Up with the Ending?"). But even if Antoinette doesn't actually die at the end, she experiences a kind of psychological death by virtue of the fact that she loses a firm grasp of her sense of self. Rochester's re-naming her Bertha and confining her to the attic destroys the woman known as Antoinette by re-drawing the boundaries of her identity.

## Three Act Plot Analysis

### Act I
After a troubled childhood and adolescence, Antoinette meets and marries Edward Rochester.

### Act II
While their honeymoon is passionate at first, it cools drastically when Rochester receives a letter containing malicious gossip about Antoinette. It becomes downright frigid when Antoinette drugs Rochester and Rochester sleeps with Antoinette's maid.

### Act III
Rochester hides Antoinette away in his estate in England, but she escapes with murderous dreams of setting fire to the whole place.

## Study Questions

1. As we mentioned in our discussion of the ending (see "What's Up with the Ending?"), the last pages of the novel are pretty open-ended. Do you think Antoinette sets fire to Thornfield Hall and commits suicide in the end? If not, what are some other possible endings?
2. Even though literary critics just call the male narrator "Rochester," the novel leaves the male narrator unnamed. Why is that?
3. What exactly was the nature of Antoinette's relationship with Sandi Cosway? Why didn't Antoinette run off with Sandi?
4. Do you think Christophine was a positive force in Antoinette's life, or do you think she was

using her? Do you think other black characters manipulated the white characters for their own ends?

5. What do you think of the representation of black characters in the book? Did you find them depicted in a stereotypically racist, psychologically flat way, or do you think there's more to the story?

6. Do you think obeah "works," at least in the world of the novel? Do you see evidence of magic or magical events? If so, where? If not, why is obeah such a factor in the novel?

7. How would the story be different if Antoinette were not a white Creole, but a black character? A colored character?

8. *Wide Sargasso Sea* tells the story of a minor character in *Jane Eyre*. If you were to write a novel about one of the minor characters in *Wide Sargasso Sea*, who would it be? What would your story be about?

## Characters

## All Characters

### Antoinette Mason Rochester Character Analysis

So…is she or isn't she? Mad, that is. Even though much of the novel is filtered through Antoinette's point of view, it's easy to read the entire novel and still have no idea who this woman *is*. Come to think of it, we're still struggling with it ourselves. Antoinette's story is certainly sad, but it's also puzzling and complicated. One thing is for sure: she seems to know how to push the right buttons. You'll find yourself alternately compelled, frustrated, and overwhelmed by her.

Now, why is that? Well, you have to admit it makes the novel a little more fun to read. Who wants to read the story of some bland goody two-shoes who angelically triumphs over evil and adversity? Antoinette is willing to dig deep into the murky side of human nature. Nature is "better than people" (I.1.3.36)? Did she just say that? This holds true for her brutal honesty with Rochester. She knows that her husband views her as inferior because she's a white Creole woman, and, no, she's not going to pretend to be calm and rational – racism is ugly and she's going to call him out on it. And she's absolutely candid about the effect that everything that's happened in her life has had on her – you know, losing her entire family, watching her mother get molested by her caretaker, listening to Rochester have sex with Amélie in the next room, getting locked up in an attic in a foreign country…

So we may not understand everything she says and does. But living in Antoinette's head for a while makes us think that she's worth taking some time to figure out. Here are a few things to mull over:

## Antoinette the Madwoman

Back to that pesky question again. Antoinette is constantly questioning who she is, but, by the end of the novel, she really seems to forget who she is. Is she insane or is there another explanation for her utterly fractured sense of self?

## Antoinette the Creole

Antoinette challenges characters both white *and* black on their views on race, particularly their treatment of white Creoles. But why doesn't she run off with Sandi, her colored lover? Does she view other black characters, like Christophine for example, as simply people to be used?

## Antoinette the Vamp

There's probably a weighty feminist tome out there on why women are called "vamps" if they're up front about their sexuality. Antoinette is called a "soucriant" in the novel, and a "vampyre" in *Jane Eyre* (II.5.2.14). Is there something off about Antoinette's sexual desires? Or is there something wrong with a culture that can't accept a woman who's frankly sexual?

## Antoinette the Zombie

Like many characters in the novel, Antoinette at times acts like a zombie, particularly at the end of Part II. But the fact that she has a close connection to the islands suggests another sense that she might be a zombie, as a "spirit of a place" that might be propitiated with offerings of flowers (remember all that frangipani in their honeymoon shack?).

## Antoinette the Victim?

You can definitely feel sorry about all the stuff that's happened to her. But how much of that is her own responsibility? Did she have any options?

## Antoinette the Dreamer

However you might feel about her as a character, you have to admit that she's got a vivid dream life, so vivid in fact that it seeps into the reality she lives in. Viewing the world through Antoinette's eyes, we get extravagant sensory detail that makes her narrative such a pleasure to read.

## Antoinette Mason Rochester Timeline and Summary

- Antoinette lives at Coulibri with her mother, Annette Cosway, and her brother, Pierre Cosway; her father has recently passed away.
- Antoinette comes across her mother's dead horse on the estate.
- Since her mother refuses to interact with her ever since her brother became ill, Antoinette seeks the company of Christophine, who sings her sad songs in *patois*.
- Antoinette becomes friends with Tia, who initially calls her racist names. Antoinette and Tia have an argument over a bet, and are no longer friends.
- Antoinette meets her mother's friends the Luttrells.
- That night, Antoinette has a nightmare where she is chased by a hostile stranger through a dark forest.

- Antoinette is a bridesmaid at her mother's wedding to Mr. Mason, and stays with Aunt Cora in Spanish Town when her mother leaves with Mr. Mason on their honeymoon.
- When the family returns to Coulibri with Mr. Mason, their house is burned down by rioters. As they are about to escape, Antoinette sees Tia and runs toward her. The next thing she knows, she's been hit by a rock, and blood is streaming down her face.
- Antoinette recovers from her injury at Aunt Cora's home in Spanish Town. Since her mother has become distraught after the death of her brother in the fire, Antoinette stays with Aunt Cora, and attends a convent school.
- While at the convent school, Mr. Mason informs Antoinette that plans are being made for her marriage.
- Antoinette dreams her nightmare for the second time. As Sister Marie Augustine comforts her, she flashes back to her mother's funeral.
- Antoinette marries Edward Rochester. They go to Granbois, Dominica, for their honeymoon.
- Antoinette and Rochester toast to their happiness. Antoinette shows him around Granbois and its environs.
- While at first wary, Antoinette eventually grows to trust Rochester and they consummate their marriage.
- Their relationship cools when Rochester receives a letter slandering Antoinette and her family.
- Antoinette fights with Amélie, her servant.
- Antoinette seeks help from Christophine, who gives her an obeah potion.
- Believing that her attempt to clear her name with Rochester has failed, Antoinette drugs him in order to seduce him.
- On discovering that Rochester has slept with her maid, Antoinette flees back to Christophine's house, where she stays for an indeterminate period of time.
- When she returns to Granbois, she confronts Rochester. The argument quickly gets out of control: she bites him and threatens him with a broken bottle.
- Antoinette is taken by Rochester back to Spanish Town.
- Antoinette is taken by Rochester to his manor in England, where she is locked up in a high room and guarded by Grace Poole.
- While confined, Antoinette has a tenuous hold on her memory and her sense of self. She dimly remembers the voyage across the sea to England, and she vaguely recalls trying to seduce a man to help her escape.
- Antoinette escapes when Grace Poole is asleep, and comes across two female guests at the house who believe she is a ghost.
- When Richard Mason visits her, Antoinette attacks him with a knife when he refuses to help her out of her marriage.
- Antoinette pulls out a red dress from the closet, which reminds her of her affair with Sandi Cosway.
- Antoinette has her nightmare for the third and last time. In the nightmare, she escapes from the room and sets fire to the house. She ends up on the roof, and jumps.
- When Antoinette wakes up, she lets herself out of the room with only a candle to light her way down the hall.

## Rochester Character Analysis

(Note: Although the novel leaves Rochester unnamed, it is common critical practice to call the unnamed male narrator Rochester, after the character in Charlotte Brontë's _Jane Eyre_.)

It's hard to view Rochester as a complete villain in this novel because he gets his own narrative in Part II. We don't get a scheming, calculating, money-grubbing monster, but someone who's really conflicted about some of the choices he's made. As the second son, he inherits nothing from his father's estate, and has to marry Antoinette if only for his own financial survival. (He could also have, you know, gotten a job, but that would have conflicted with his gentlemanly pretensions…) And he's understandably humiliated by his situation. To his credit, he seems touched by Antoinette, perhaps seeing in her vulnerability a mirror of his own.

But he does end up doing some pretty awful things. He treats Antoinette horribly without giving her time to reply to Daniel's allegations. He sleeps with the maid – on his honeymoon, with his wife in the next room. He gets Antoinette declared mad and locks her up in his attic.

So how does a man who doesn't seem particularly evil end up living the rough equivalent of five straight seasons of _Days of Our Lives_? One huge hurdle that Rochester can't seem to overcome is his Englishness. In fact, because he's got something of an inferiority complex – second son, married a girl for her money, stuck out in a colony instead of hipper London – his Englishness is all the more important to him to shore up his ego.

Everything about the Caribbean rubs Rochester the wrong way because it isn't rational, civilized, domesticated, and scientific – to him. The Caribbean has all kinds of fantastic elements – magical elements like obeah, racial and cultural diversity, exotic natural beauty. And the women. Fiery, strong-willed women like Antoinette and Christophine. Instead of opening up to this world, Rochester exaggerates his own Englishness, growing more coldly rational and condescending as things get more and more out of control.

Even so, he seems conflicted to the very end, experiencing a twinge of regret and nostalgia as he and Antoinette leave Granbois. He's not a man entirely comfortable with exploiting other people, and not entirely comfortable with his own claim that he never loved Antoinette. Otherwise, why would he hate her so much? You might find yourself wondering what it would have taken to save their relationship, but that would have been a very different novel indeed.

## Rochester Timeline and Summary

- Rochester and Antoinette arrive in Granbois, Dominica for their honeymoon.
- In a flashback, Rochester thinks of how he'd been in Jamaica for only a month before he married Antoinette, and he'd been ill for most of that month.
- Rochester and Antoinette toast to happiness with a couple of glasses of rum.
- Antoinette shows Rochester to Mr. Mason's former dressing room, where Rochester writes a letter to his father.

- In a flashback, Rochester remembers that Antoinette had almost called off the wedding, but he had gone to her to convince her to marry him.
- Rochester gets to know Antoinette as they share meals together and tour the estate.
- Eventually, Rochester consummates his marriage with Antoinette.
- Rochester receives a letter from a man claiming to be Daniel Cosway. The letter is filled with malicious attacks on Antoinette and her family.
- Stunned by the letter, Rochester goes for a walk and, when he returns, he breaks up a fight between Antoinette and Amélie.
- Rochester goes out for another walk. This time, he gets lost in a clearing in a dark forest where he finds an obeah offering of flowers. A girl sees him and runs away, thinking that he's a ghost.
- Rochester receives a second letter from Daniel and confronts him. He refuses to be blackmailed by Daniel.
- Rochester discusses Daniel's allegations with Antoinette. He sips some wine offered by Antoinette, and slowly loses consciousness.
- Rochester wakes up and realizes he's been drugged. He goes out for a walk by the clearing where he'd gotten lost the first time.
- When he returns, he sees Amélie and sleeps with her. When she wakes up, he offers her money. As she leaves, he hears Antoinette leaving at the same time.
- When Antoinette returns, Rochester has an argument with her that quickly escalates. She bites him and threatens him with a broken bottle.
- Christophine intervenes, and, when Antoinette retreats, Christophine confronts Rochester about his behavior. Rochester is feeling groggy throughout their conversation until she mentions that, for money, she's willing to take care of Antoinette. Rochester cuts their conversation short.
- Rochester decides to leave Granbois for Spanish Town and have Antoinette declared insane.
- On the sea voyage to England, Rochester discovers that Antoinette is attempting to seduce a young man on the boat into helping her escape.
- Rochester confines Antoinette to a room in his English manor.

## Christophine Character Analysis

Christophine, Annette's servant and Antoinette's nurse, is one character where a first-person point of view might have helped. (For first person narratives, we get Antoinette, Rochester, and (drum roll)…Grace Poole.*Grace Poole*. Sigh.)

On the one hand, Christophine seems to be a benevolent force in Antoinette's life. She becomes a substitute mom when Antoinette's mother goes off the deep end. When Antoinette and Rochester's marriage hits the rocks, Christophine is filled with earthy nuggets of inspiration like, "A man don't treat you good, pick up your skirt and walk out" and "Have spunks and do battle for yourself." (This woman deserves her own VH1 Celebreality show.) And, for Antoinette, Christophine represents somebody who's completely comfortable with her racial identity, and contributes to Antoinette's own identification with black Caribbean culture.

And yet...why is Christophine such a shady character? It may have something to do with the fact that she was imprisoned for practicing obeah, called voodoo in the French colonies (see our discussion of obeah in "The Supernatural," under "Themes," for more on why obeah was considered politically dangerous). The fact that she's from Martinique, a French colony, makes her doubly suspect in the English colonies where the novel takes place. Despite Antoinette's rapturous devotion, we get glimmers of a woman who doesn't seem to have Antoinette's best interest at heart.

Why, for example, was Mr. Cosway so fond of her, giving her a house of her own near Granbois? Why does Christophine stick around with the Cosways when Mr. Cosway dies? Why didn't she come in to say good night to Antoinette on the night the estate burned down? Why does Christophine give Antoinette the obeah powder when it's pretty obvious from what Antoinette says that she has every intention of drugging Rochester, regardless of whether he accepts her explanation or not? And why is everyone, black and white, so afraid of Christophine? We never find out exactly why Christophine was jailed, and both Antoinette and Rochester note in their narratives that Christophine is constantly mumbling things that they don't understand. Is Rochester right? Is Christophine just out to exploit Antoinette for her money?

Whether you believe in Christophine's obeah powers or not, she's a formidable character, definitely not to be taken lightly.

## Christophine Timeline and Summary

- Antoinette seeks Christophine's company when her mother ignores her after Pierre falls ill.
- Christophine discovers that the daughter of her friend Maillotte, Tia, has been taunting Antoinette and arranges for Tia and Antoinette to become friends.
- Christophine walks in when Antoinette thinks she may have found an obeah charm in her room; Christophine acts like nothing is wrong.
- Christophine does not show up to wish Antoinette a good night as she usually does on the night that the Coulibri estate burns down, but shows up later that night when everybody in the house has gathered. During the fire, Christophine helps to put out the fire.
- At Granbois, Christophine is among the servants who welcome Antoinette and Rochester.
- Christophine serves Antoinette and Rochester coffee in bed on their first morning.
- After Rochester receives a letter from Daniel Cosway/Boyd, Christophine leaves Granbois, saying that she doesn't want to come between Antoinette and Rochester. As she leaves, she threatens Amélie.
- Christophine gives Antoinette an obeah potion to give to Rochester.
- Antoinette arrives at Christophine's after giving the potion to Rochester, with disastrous results. Christophine returns to Granbois with Antoinette, and yells at Rochester.

## Annette Cosway Mason Character Analysis

A native of Martinique like Christophine, Annette is Antoinette's mother, and functions in the novel as an awful shadow of what's to come for her daughter. Unlucky in love – check. Discriminated against for being a Creole woman – check. Manipulated by Christophine (probably) – check. Physically attacks her husband – check. Gets declared insane – check. Gets confined for being insane – check. Annette's death even takes place off stage; we never learn how Annette actually died. We just learn about Annette's funeral in an offhand comment by Antoinette as she drinks some cocoa. The fact that we never learn how Annette's life actually ends is a wink at the novel's ending, which is similarly reticent as to how Antoinette's life ends.

And yes, their names are almost the same – but *almost*. While Antoinette may have inherited many elements of her mother's unfortunate destiny, the fact that there are still differences between the two women's lives suggests that, despite what all the gossip-mongers say, Antoinette didn't "inherit" her mental illness from her mother, but perhaps other factors – social, historical, cultural, but definitely not genetic or racial – played into their mutual fates.

## Annette Cosway Mason Timeline and Summary

- After her husband dies, Annette tries to keep things together on the Cosway estate.
- She goes out riding on her horse – the next day, her daughter Antoinette finds the horse poisoned. Annette suspects that her servant Godfrey knows what happened.
- Annette calls in a doctor to examine her son, Pierre. Although the novel doesn't state the doctor's diagnosis, Annette is devastated and barely talks to anyone, let alone her daughter. She wanders the house talking to herself.
- Annette sees Antoinette one day wearing a dirty dress on the same day that she meets the Luttrells. Annette sells her jewelry to buy them both new dresses. Annette begins to socialize again, this time with the Luttrells.
- Annette marries Mr. Mason, a wealthy plantation owner. They go on a honeymoon while her children stay with Aunt Cora.
- Back at Coulibri, she tries to convince Mr. Mason that it's too dangerous for them there. Mr. Mason dismisses her.
- As the rioters gather outside the house, Annette notices smoke coming from Pierre's room and runs in to save her son. As they leave Coulibri, she tries to save her parrot, Coco, but Mr. Mason pulls her out, kicking and screaming.
- Annette yells at Mr. Mason and blames him for the death of her son and Coulibri. She is overheard by Antoinette.
- Mr. Mason leaves Annette in a house outside Spanish Town to be cared for. When Antoinette visits Annette, Antoinette sees a man give Annette alcohol and molest Annette.
- Annette's funeral is attended by Antoinette.

## Mr. Mason Character Analysis

Mr. Mason, a wealthy planter and Annette's second husband, is mainly in the novel to anticipate Rochester. Like Rochester, Mr. Mason doesn't comprehend racial relations on the island, and dismisses Annette's warnings as unfounded. While he does not marry Annette for her money (because she has none), Mr. Mason also finds that, like Rochester, his attraction to his wife quickly sours when he discovers – or decides, depending on how you look at it – that she's mentally ill and has her confined under inhumane conditions. Mr. Mason may or may not have genuinely cared for Antoinette's security, but his belief that a woman is best off under the care of an English gentleman backfires, tragically.

## Pierre Cosway Character Analysis

Poor Pierre, Antoinette's little brother, doesn't get much play in the novel. He doesn't talk or do anything; his main function in the novel is to get ill and die. Both his illness and his death end up driving his mother insane with grief. It's not clear why Annette should care so much more for Pierre than Antoinette, but given the way that women are treated in the novel, it may have something to do with Pierre's being the only male in the family.

## Tia Character Analysis

With friends like Tia, who needs enemies? Antoinette first meets Tia when Tia followed her home, hurling racist insults at her – the basis for a sound friendship, right? Of course not. While they do become friends, the friendship quickly shatters over a petty bet and they go back to hurling racist insults at each other. But, in the last scene at Coulibri, we never see Tia actually throw the rock that hurts Antoinette, either because Antoinette has repressed that memory (it's her point of view in the narrative) or because the novel wants there to be the slim chance that someone else threw the rock.

For Antoinette, Tia is the image of someone who is completely in tune with the island and with her black community in a way that Antoinette could never be, however much she desires it. Antoinette's constant reference to Tia as her reflection, even in the last dream at Thornfield Hall, suggests that her desire for the wholeness that Tia represents is a driving force in her life.

## Sandi Cosway Character Analysis

Sandi Cosway is the son of Alexander Cosway, Antoinette's father's son by another woman. Unlike Daniel Cosway/Boyd, Alexander Cosway and his son are members of colored society who are accepted by some sections of white society; they are even informally acknowledged by Mr. Cosway. Sandi appears briefly in the novel: he saves Antoinette from some harassing children, he teaches her to throw a rock…and he's also the love of her life. Antoinette never explains why she never married Sandi, but the novel suggests that the fact that he was colored

was an insuperable barrier for her family and perhaps for herself.

## Richard Mason Character Analysis

Richard Mason, Antoinette's stepbrother, helps Mr. Mason fulfill his goal of marrying Antoinette to an Englishman after Mr. Mason dies, and refuses to help Antoinette even when he sees how she is imprisoned in Rochester's attic. He's basically in the novel to represent yet another male figure who exploits Antoinette's vulnerable position as a white Creole woman.

## Aunt Cora Character Analysis

Antoinette's Aunt Cora appears to be the one person who has Antoinette's best interests at heart. But, because she's a woman, she has only limited resources to draw on to help Antoinette. While she berates Richard and makes the very valid point that Antoinette's fortune needs to be legally protected, she can only offer Antoinette a few rings to sell just in case Antoinette gets into trouble. Like Antoinette, Aunt Cora also marries an Englishman and moves to England, but is able to move freely between Jamaica and England once her husband dies.

## Amélie Character Analysis

Amélie, Antoinette's maid at Granbois, sleeps with Rochester after he is poisoned by Antoinette. But she's not just a saucy vixen. Like Tia, she taunts Antoinette with racist slurs, and Rochester notes a disturbing similarity between her features and Antoinette's. Amélie is in the story just as much to stress the commonalities between Antoinette and Tia as she is to wreck Antoinette's marriage, precisely by taking Antoinette's place in Rochester's bed.

## Daniel Cosway/Boyd Character Analysis

Since the novel never tells us who's telling the truth, we're giving Antoinette the benefit of the doubt here and calling this character Daniel Cosway/Boyd. Claiming to be the illegitimate son of Mr. Cosway and one of his slaves, Daniel sends a spiteful letter to Rochester with the intention of destroying Antoinette's marriage and blackmailing Rochester to keep the scandal quiet. While at times Daniel puffs himself up as an educated and moral man, at other times he debases himself before Rochester and embraces the idea that he's an intellectual inferior because of his race. The blend of self-aggrandizement and self-hatred makes this character a particularly vivid example of the twisted logic of racist thinking.

## Grace Poole Character Analysis

Grace Poole, Antoinette's guard and nurse at Thornfield Hall, gets some brief play at the end of

the novel – even a short narrative of her own. Even though it seems kind of random, it does make sense that Grace has her own story. In keeping with the novel's general project of telling the untold story behind *Jane Eyre*, Grace Poole gets a chance to explain why she would ever take a job where she's paid to be stuck in a room all alone with a so-called lunatic. In *Jane Eyre*, Jane mistakes Grace for Antoinette (called Bertha in *Jane Eyre*), so Grace is a kind of double for Antoinette. Grace's identification and sympathy with Antoinette's story shows how Antoinette's story can be applied to women of all nationalities. As Grace says, "the world outside…can be a black and cruel world to a woman" (III.1.2).

## Sister Marie Augustine Character Analysis

Sister Marie Augustine is Antoinette's favorite nun at the convent school in Spanish Town, Jamaica. She comforts Antoinette when Antoinette is tormented by religious conundrums and nightmares.

## Godfrey Character Analysis

Godfrey is one of the Cosway servants who remained with the estate after Mr. Cosway passed away. He's a morose fellow who Annette suspects of knowing how her horse got poisoned.

## Myra Character Analysis

Myra is a servant who shows up after Mr. Mason and Annette get married. Aunt Cora suspects her of being a spy who tells the former slaves in the area about Mr. Mason's plan to import laborers from the East Indies. She is also Pierre's nurse, but goes missing once the fire starts at Coulibri.

## Baptiste Character Analysis

Baptiste is the head of the servants at Granbois. His respectful treatment of Rochester turns to disdain after Rochester sleeps with Amélie.

## Hilda Character Analysis

Hilda, a servant at Granbois, is a young girl who's a mini-Amélie – all the malicious giggling but without the sex.

# Character Roles

### Protagonist
*Antoinette*
Antoinette is clearly the character around which the novel's events revolve. Her first-person narratives in Parts I, II, and III frame Rochester's and Grace Poole's narratives.

### Antagonist
*Rochester*
While Antoinette encounters a lot of hostility in the novel, none really matches the drubbing she gets from Rochester. The fact that he makes passionate love to her in the beginning only magnifies the hurt he inflicts after he receives the damning letter from Daniel Cosway/Boyd. And did we mention that he locks her up in his attic?

### Antagonist
*Christophine*
From Antoinette's childhood on, Christophine serves as a source of comfort and some pretty solid relationship advice. Her behavior at times, however, does call into question how pure her intentions really are.

### Foil
*Tia to Antoinette*
Antoinette refers to Tia in Parts I and III as her reflection. Despite their racial differences, Tia represents how Antoinette, as a Creole, identifies more strongly with the black Caribbean community than with white society.

# Character Clues

### Race
Race is integral to the way these characters interact in the novel. Often, the first thing we learn about characters is their race because it's the first thing that Antoinette and Rochester notice about a person, and we get everything from their point of view. The novel draws on racial categories specific to nineteenth-century Jamaica:

**Black:** A person descended from the African slaves imported by British and French plantation owners. Christophine, Godfrey, Amélie, and most of the servants are black. Despite the Emancipation Act of 1833, blacks in Jamaica are still an economic and political under-class at the time of the novel.

**White** (also called *béké*): A person of European origin. Edward Rochester and Mr. Mason are white characters. But then there are the Creoles…

**Creole:** In the nineteenth century, "Creole" does *not* mean someone of mixed racial origin, but a white person of European origin born in the Caribbean. Antoinette, her mother, and her brother

are all Creole characters. Technically they're white, so you'll often hear them referred to as "white Creoles." But even though they're white, it was commonly believed that the island climate "contaminated" their race, making them lesser whites, so to speak. You'll notice that the characters are called "white cockroaches" or "white niggers," derogatory terms for white Creoles.

**Colored:** A person of mixed racial origin, both black and white and/or Creole. Their social position is similar to that of blacks, but because of their mixed racial origin, there is more possibility for economic mobility. Sandi Cosway and his father are examples of colored characters.

**Carib:** Indigenous to the Caribbean. Although we don't meet anyone clearly identified as Carib, some characters such as Antoinette have a strong belief that neither whites nor blacks have prior claim to the islands because the islands were already inhabited by the Caribs and other indigenous peoples. The name of the town Massacre invokes this history (see our discussion in "Setting").

### Speech and Dialogue

Since the events are told from a character's point of view, speech and dialogue are critical to our understanding of the characters. We get scene after scene of clashing perspectives, where the attempt to have a real dialogue, if there is one, often fails miserably. Think, for example, of Antoinette's attempt to clear her name with Rochester, or Annette's attempt to convince Mr. Mason that it is no longer safe for them at Coulibri. In addition, stray phrases of *patois*, the dialectal English spoken by the black Caribbeans, and the pompous diction associated with the white English settler class shape the social world of the novel.

### Type of Being

Whether there's any real magic going on in the world of the novel is up for debate. But the novel keeps presenting characters that are like zombies, ghosts, or puppets. Such beings freak us out because they look human but are not; they're on the border between life and death, the animate and inanimate. Antoinette's doll-like demeanor after her relationship with Rochester is ruined, Annette's zombie-esque behavior after she finds out her son is ill, Rochester's trance-like state during his dialogue with Christophine, and even Pierre's mysterious illness all mark instances where the characters are taken out of their comfort zone and become transformed.

## Literary Devices

## Symbols, Imagery, Allegory

### The Land

Antoinette explains to Rochester that she "loved" the land because she "had nothing else to love" (II.6.3.36). You could say the land is itself a character in the novel. The description of the land sets the tone for the whole drama, as it reflects the various characters' emotions – lust and

innocence, hope and despair, love and fear. From the lush gardens of Coulibri in Part I to the dense forests of Granbois in Part II, the land pulses with Technicolor brilliance. It's no wonder that Antoinette's only whiff of happiness in Part III occurs outside, in the English countryside, instead of in the miserable little room in which she's imprisoned. (For a fuller discussion of specific passages, see our discussion of "Contrasting Regions" under "Themes.")

### Birds and Beasts

The birds and animals in *Wide Sargasso Sea* are usually allegories for the struggles of the individual characters. Coco isn't just a pyromaniacal parrot who ends up saving everyone's lives, but a voice for Antoinette's own conflicted identity when he calls out, " *Qui est là?*" Cockroaches obviously echo the term "white cockroach," a derogatory epithet applied to white Creoles, but fireflies and moths also populate the novel's emotional life. A black-and-white goat appears after Rochester speaks with Daniel, as a symbol perhaps of Daniel's racial status or his moral duplicity, or Rochester's ambivalence regarding Daniel. And so forth, and so on. Like the land, the birds and the beasts of *Wide Sargasso Sea* are veritable actors in the drama of the novel, the extras in the background who sometimes steal the scene.

### Red Dress, White Dress

To all the fashionistas out there, you know how you feel when you've got *the* dress on. It could be vintage couture or an absolute steal you picked up at some post-post-clearance sale, but it fits you just right in all the right places. Men want you and women want to be you – or know where you bought it. For Antoinette, that dress is her red dress. It symbolizes her femininity, and, infused with the fragrance of Caribbean flowers and spices, it also symbolizes her Creole identity. It has an almost magical power to revive her in Part III, and the fact that it looks like a fire when it's spread out on the floor suggests one way that she can wreak her revenge on Rochester. The white dress, on the other hand, is associated with male dominance, rather than feminine chastity or wedded bliss. White is the color favored by her mother, and white is the color of the dress Antoinette wears in her nightmare.

### Fire

Fire in the novel is associated with rebellion, both political and emotional. In Part I, ex-slaves set fire to Coulibri as an expression of their discontent, partly with Mr. Mason's plan to import slaves from the East Indies. Antoinette's dream of setting fire to Thornfield Hall in Part III suggests a parallel between the ex-slaves' protest and her own protest against Rochester and the patriarchal system he embodies.

## Setting

### 1830s Coulibri, near Spanish Town, Jamaica; 1840s Granbois, near Massacre, Dominica; and Thornfield Hall, England

While the novel never gives us the exact year, we know that the novel is set in Jamaica at some point after 1834. (By the end of Part I, Antoinette mentions that she enters the convent in 1839 [I.2.4.1].) While in *Jane Eyre* the events take place in the 1800s, Rhys moves the events up thirty years during a time of social and political upheaval in Jamaica, which is at the time a

British colony.

The novel opens a few years after Britain passed the Emancipation Act of 1833, which went into effect a year later (fifteen years before the French, and nearly thirty years before the Americans, we should add). While slaveholders were promised compensation for freeing their slaves, many slaveholders, like Antoinette's father, Mr. Cosway, and her neighbor, Mr. Luttrell, never received payment and were ruined. The newly freed slaves, on the other hand, are stuck in an apprenticeship system for four years following the act which is just as bad as slavery: they're forced to apprentice for their former owners, and the punishment for escaping was just as bad as the punishment under slavery. Not surprisingly, the former slaves continue to bear a major grudge against their former owners, and riots are common. Because so many plantations go under, many English investors arrive at the island seeking a good deal – people like the Luttrells and Mr. Mason, and, indirectly, Rochester. It's tough to pity the former slaveholders, we know, and one important question is whether you feel that Rhys's novel seems at all nostalgic for that period in Jamaican history.

In Part II, the novel moves to Granbois, the Cosway estate outside Massacre, Dominica. Unlike Jamaica, Dominica has flip-flopped between British and French imperial control over the years. At the time, it is also known as a stronghold of the Caribs, an indigenous Caribbean people. In the past, the Caribs have periodically staged insurgencies against the British and the French. The name of the town "Massacre" refers to a particularly bloody massacre of the Caribs, but nobody who lives there remembers the massacre itself. It's just another creepy name, as far as they're concerned. ( Learn more.) The name "Granbois," meaning "big tree" or "big wood," underscores the creepiness of the locale. There's nothing wrong with big trees in general, but in the novel, big trees echo the dark forests of Antoinette's nightmares.

The novel ends in Thornfield Hall, England, Rochester's home. Unlike Parts I and II, where we get lush descriptions of the Caribbean, we don't see much of England since most of it is from Antoinette's point of view, who's locked up in the attic. It's no wonder that she thinks she's stuck in a world made of cardboard, and not in England. Her belief that she's living in a world made of paper is a not-so-subtle hint that the novel has returned to the primary landscape of _Jane Eyre_, the Victorian novel which it freely adapts.


## Narrator Point of View


### First Person
The novel is a patchwork of various first-person narratives, told directly to the reader (Antoinette, Rochester) or told to another character (Grace Poole). Moreover, the narratives often relate the same events from different perspectives. For example, the events in Antoinette's childhood are relayed in Antoinette's narrative in Part I, then told from various gossipy points of view (Daniel, Amélie, Christophine, among them) to Rochester, then Antoinette again retells the story in an abbreviated form to Rochester. In all this story-telling, the novel never gives us access to the truth of what happens from the point of view of some impartial or omniscient observer, so it's easy to get lost in an endless spiral of who says what

about whom.

## Genre

### Coming of Age, Historical Fiction, Horror or Gothic Fiction, Literary Fiction, Modernism

We've got a lot of genres here, but they can all really be explained by the genre of "literary fiction." *Wide Sargasso Sea* is very in-your-face about the fact that it's tackling one of the classics of Victorian fiction, Charlotte Brontë's *Jane Eyre*. Its language is loaded with allusions to everything from the Bible on up to Thomas De Quincey's *Confessions of an Opium Eater*, peppered with a few popular Caribbean and music hall songs. This kind of self-conscious literary riffing is pretty much what you get with "literary fiction," a genre that aspires to be stylistically innovative and shuns commercial appeal.

As part and parcel of this stylistic innovation, the novel subverts other literary genres: enter "Coming of Age," "Historical Fiction," "Horror and Gothic Fiction," and "Modernism." Usually in a coming-of-age story, we get some kind of maturity as a character transitions from childhood to adulthood, but with *Wide Sargasso Sea*, surprise, we don't get maturity (unless burning down a house is your idea of maturity).

In "Historical Fiction," we usually get some concrete historical dates, personages, and events to get our bearings, but the novel makes only sparing references to historical events that are, nevertheless, absolutely critical to our understanding of the novel (see the brief mention of the Emancipation Act on the very first page).

The novel certainly has its fair share of ghosts and creepy houses, the mainstays of "Horror and Gothic Fiction," but the novel is only scary if you believe that Christophine can work supernatural wonders.

Finally, Jean Rhys's previous novels were all in the high Modernist vein – some famous ones include *Good Morning, Midnight* and *Voyage in the Dark*. They are very stylized, very innovative, very complex, but largely set in bohemian Paris or London. By setting the majority of her novel in the Caribbean, Rhys makes Modernist style speak to the many important social and political issues of the time.

## Tone

### Critical

Despite the sympathy Rhys expressed for Antoinette's situation in her letters, in the actual novel the prevailing attitude is critical. It's not that the novel disapproves of anyone necessarily, but it's trying to evaluate everything with a critical eye. There are no heroines or villains in the novel. The novel seeks to create a balanced view of the forces that push and pull each and every single character – it seeks to understand, not to praise or condemn. Rochester may be a

loser for marrying a girl for her money, then locking her up in his attic, but the novel tries to give Rochester the benefit of the doubt by letting him tell the story from his perspective. Instead of an evil guy, we get someone who is vulnerable, naïve, sometimes well-intentioned, and not particularly brilliant, trying to make the best of an overwhelming situation. Antoinette may be the heroine and the inspiration for the story, but the novel also shows how her own limited way of looking at the world contributes to her unhappiness.

## Writing Style

### Sophisticated yet readable

We're not talking super-hard vocabulary or weird syntax here. The language in *Wide Sargasso Sea* is simple, but every word is weighted with enormous significance. Take the first line for example:

*They say when trouble comes close ranks, and so the white people did. But we were not in their ranks.*

There's nothing in those two sentences that a fifth-grader couldn't understand, but they open up a whole world for the reader. With the first line, you know you're not getting a comedy. You're in a time and place when "trouble," whatever it is, is a common occurrence. You're entering a situation that calls for a community to come together, and in the novel's world, that community has to be racially homogenous. You know with the next line that the narrator's family doesn't fit within the category of "white people," and, as the novel goes on, you know that just because they're not "white," doesn't mean that they're black, either – they're Creoles. Throughout the novel, everyday language is masterfully engineered to describe extraordinary situations.

## What's Up With the Title?

The title of the novel refers to the Sargasso Sea, a vast area of the northern Atlantic Ocean which is home to sargassum, a kind of seaweed. The Sargasso Sea is legendary for being an oceanic black hole, where ships get ensnared by huge forests of floating seaweed, or drift helplessly when the wind ceases to blow.

The title invites the reader to consider how the characters can be thought of as trapped in their own Sargasso Seas. They may be suspended in the murky passage between two worlds, between England and Jamaica, for example, or between racial identities, as Antoinette struggles with her white Creole heritage. But the terrors of the Sargasso Sea are also largely mythical, the product of sailor lore rather than historical or scientific fact. By linking itself to this mythical tradition, the novel asks the reader to consider the role of stories and fictions in the characters' lives, particularly when it comes to encountering experiences that are foreign, alien, and strange.

## What's Up With the Ending?

To answer this question, we first have to figure out what the ending *isn't* . It is certainly true that *Wide Sargasso Sea* is a kind of prequel to Charlotte Brontë's *Jane Eyre*. (For more on the *Jane Eyre* connection, see "In A Nutshell.") But we can't take for granted that what holds true for *Jane Eyre* holds true for *Wide Sargasso Sea* as well. Thus, while in *Jane Eyre*, Antoinette (called Bertha in *Jane Eyre*) sets Thornfield Hall on fire and leaps to her death, in *Wide Sargasso Sea* we never actually see Antoinette doing any of this *except in her dream*. In fact, the novel's last lines are ambiguous:

*Now at last I know why I was brought here and what I have to do. There must have been a draught for the flame flickered and I thought it was out. But I shielded it with my hand and it burned up again to light me along the dark passage.*

It is certainly possible that Antoinette will set fire to Thornfield Hall, but this becomes only one possibility among others. For "passage," the very last word of the novel, asks us to consider all of the different ways that Antoinette is passing from one state to another – physically, certainly, but psychologically, culturally, even politically as well.

Does Antoinette's appeal to black characters such as Tia and Christophine in her dream imply that she rejects her white Creole identity for a black Caribbean one, symbolized by her setting the house on fire just as the black rioters did to Coulibri earlier in the novel? Then why not show her actually doing this? Why keep it in a dream?

Or is the "passage" a passage into selfhood, a way of recovering from the psychological trauma that troubled her from childhood and into adulthood with her relationship with Rochester? As Part III progresses, she transitions from having no knowledge of who she is to remembering everything. Thus the fact that she has dreamed her dream for the last time, a dream that incorporates scenes from her entire life, could be a way of overcoming a life-long, self-destructive pattern of behavior.

Or is the passage a literary one, a passage that signals Antoinette's final emergence from behind the shadowy fiction of Bertha Mason in *Jane Eyre*? With this view, Antoinette is neither a political heroine or psychologically cured, but just a dramatic representation of how voices are silenced in the great texts of English literature.

These are just a few of the possible outcomes, so go ahead – get lost in the novel for a while and see what you come up with. Appropriately for a novel that is itself a re-reading of a literary classic, the ending of *Wide Sargasso Sea* invites endless re-readings and interpretations.

# Did You Know?

## Trivia

- Many elements in the novel parallel Rhys's own life. Like Antoinette, Rhys came from a white Creole family; her mother was a third-generation white Creole and her father was a Welsh doctor. Her great-grandfather, John Potter Lockhart, bought Geneva plantation in 1824, but much of it was destroyed during the riots following emancipation in 1844. Although she lived in England and Europe for most of her adult life, she was much affected when she visited her ancestral home in 1936 after it had burned down in 1930. (Source)
- Rhys worked as a chorus girl, among other jobs, before she became a writer. She was mentored by Modernist writer Ford Maddox Ford, with whom she eventually had an affair. (Source)
- Rhys considered *The First Mrs. Rochester*, *Creole*, and *Le Revenant* as other titles for *Wide Sargasso Sea*. (Source)
- The Sargasso Sea is integral to the general mystery surrounding the Bermuda Triangle, an area in the Atlantic Ocean where many ships and planes have reportedly been lost. In one story, the *Ellen Austin* (a schooner) found a stranded schooner in 1881. Some of the crew members boarded the stranded ship and both ships sailed together for port. Two days later, the *Ellen Austin* saw the stranded schooner again, weaving about in an irregular way. When boarded yet again, the ship showed no traces of the crew. (Source)
- Coco the pyro-parrot may not be such a random character after all. In 1816, a law was passed in Jamaica that forbade slaves from possessing parrot beaks, among other things, because they were used in obeah witchcraft. (Source)

## Steaminess Rating

### R

Antoinette and Rochester's relationship is passionately physical at one point – after all, they're newly-wedded. As their relationship deteriorates, Antoinette uses sex to manipulate Rochester, and Rochester has sex with her maid to get back at her. There are also fleeting references to Antoinette's past and present affairs. There's a lot of sex in the book, but it's presented metaphorically, not explicitly – the sex takes place discreetly off the page. Thus, it's an R.

## Allusions and Cultural References

### Literary and Philosophical References

- Charlotte Brontë, *Jane Eyre* – the novel as a whole tells the story of Bertha Mason, a character in *Jane Eyre*, but here are the explicit allusions: II.5.2.14; II.6.6.41; III.6.1; III.7.4
- Lord Byron (II.1.2.38)
- Sir Walter Scott (II.1.2.38)
- Thomas de Quincey, *Confessions of an Opium Eater* (II.1.2.38)
- François de Malherbe, "Consolation à M. du Périer" (II.3.3.19)
- William Shakespeare, *Othello* (II.3.5.40)
- William Shakespeare, *Macbeth* (II.7.4)

### Biblical References

- Genesis (I.1.2.2; II.6.2.5)
- Matthew (I.2.5.3; II.1.1.32; II.5.2.30)
- Deuteronomy (II.6.2.3)

## Best of the Web

## Websites

### Jean Rhys and Dominica
http://www.lennoxhonychurch.com/jeanrhysbio.cfm
This site provides biographical detail on Jean Rhys, with special emphasis on the impact that the history and landscape of Dominica had on her work.

### Critical Approaches to *Wide Sargasso Sea*
http://www.qub.ac.uk/schools/SchoolofEnglish/imperial/carib/carib.htm
This site provides specific historical data relevant to the novel, as well as a summary of a few useful theoretical approaches.

## Movies or TV Productions

### *Wide Sargasso Sea*, 1993
http://www.imdb.com/title/tt0108565/
The cover photo of a man burying his face in a woman's heaving bosom, not to mention the NC-17 rating for the unedited version, says it all.

### *Wide Sargasso Sea*, 2006
http://www.imdb.com/title/tt0828462/
A somewhat more modest adaptation made for British television.

## Historical Documents

Obeah
http://scholar.library.miami.edu/slaves/Religion/religion.html
This site provides excellent historical background on the practice of obeah, including interesting eyewitness accounts and quotes from relevant legislative acts.

## Images

Jean Rhys
http://www.english.uwosh.edu/core/images/rhys.gif
A famous photograph of Jean Rhys

Spanish Town, Jamaica 1820
http://www.jamaica-gleaner.com/pages/history/images/spanish1.jpg
Spanish Town roughly fifteen years before the events of the novel take place.

Printed in Great Britain
by Amazon